PATHFINDER PILOT

The Search
for
Selwyn Alcock DFC

ROGER PERKINS

£6.50 UK

PATHFINDER PILOT
The Search for Selwyn Alcock DFC

By the same author
(for Kenneth Mason, Havant, Hampshire)
Gunfire in Barbary (1982) (with Capt K J Douglas-Morris)

(for Picton Publishing, Chippenham, Wiltshire)
Angels in Blue Jackets (1983) (with J W Wilson)
The Kashmir Gate (1983)
The Punjab Mail Murder (1986)
Operation Paraquat – The Battle for South Georgia – 1982 (1986)
The Amritsar Legacy (1989)

(privately)
Regiments of the Empire – A Bibliography (1989)

Researched, compiled and published privately by the author
Typeset by Impressit, Newton Abbot, Devon
Artwork by A&B Creative Services, Kingskerswell, Devon
Produced and printed by Abbot Litho Press, Newton Abbot, Devon

Contents

The success of a large-scale night raid by the RAF is in increasing measure dependent on the conscientious flying of the Pathfinder crews. The frictionless functioning of the attack is only possible when the turning points on the inward and outward courses, as well as the target itself, are properly marked. Lately, these attacks have been compressed into about four minutes for each wave averaging 120-150 aircraft...

Whereas the attacks of the British heavy bombers during the years 1942-1943 lasted over an hour, the duration of the attack has been progressively shortened so that today a raid of 800-900 aircraft is compressed into twenty minutes at the most...

In spite of the increased danger of collision or dropping bombs on other aircraft which must be taken into account, the aim has been achieved of allowing the (German) defences, the Commands as well as the defence weapons themselves, only a fraction of the time available to them during raids in the past. The realisation of these aims was made possible by the conscientious work of the Pathfinder group and by the high training standard (especially regarding navigation) of the crews...

Extracts from a Luftwaffe Intelligence report, dated March 1944.

Foreword

by

Group Captain T G 'Hamish' Mahaddie

DSO, DFC, AFC & bar, CzMC, C Eng, FRAeS, RAF (retd)

Whilst I feel that I am a poor substitute for the late John Searby in presenting a Foreword to the chronicle of Flight Lieutenant Selwyn Alcock, my involvement with the Pathfinder Force does permit me to indulge in a commentary upon his life and times.

The Pathfinder Force (PFF) was formed in August 1942 at the direct order of the Air Ministry. Appointed to head it was Don Bennett, an Australian and brilliant former airline pilot. His job was to find a way of guiding our bombers to a chosen target and ensuring that their bombs all fell on the same spot and at more or less the same time. This move was not at first welcomed by our chief, 'Bomber' Harris, or by some of his senior officers. They viewed the creation of an elite force as a drain on the quality of the other front-line squadrons. The first five squadrons selected for the PFF, the pioneers, needed to prove a point.

By January of 1943 there was enough evidence to justify an expansion of the Force and it became No 8 (PFF) Group. This meant transferring in many more aircrew from other Groups. Instead of releasing only good crews, some of the main force Groups took the chance to unload troublesome or inefficient crews. In some cases, transfer to No 8 Group was treated as a 'punishment posting'.

A few weeks later, in March, I was hi-jacked from 7 Squadron, then based at RAF Oakington, and thrust into the midst of Don Bennett's headquarters at Huntingdon. Appointed Group Training Inspector, I was given a free hand to put a stop to what had been going on, and to select the best crews I could find in Bomber Command. Having joined the Royal Air Force in 1928, having passed through Halton and having qualified pre-war as a Sergeant Pilot, I thought I probably knew a few tricks of my own. The fact that I had just completed fifty-eight operational sorties, twenty-five of them as a Pathfinder, was an added advantage.

From the beginning, I borrowed a phrase from Lord Trenchard when he had introduced the Halton Apprentice scheme in 1922: 'The best is only just good enough'. My appointment brought the flow of indifferent crews to an abrupt end. The job then was to attract volunteers of outstanding quality, and to make sure that none of those who wanted to join the PFF were being blocked by Squadron commanders who were reluctant to lose them. At first, I had to counter a great deal of criticism from the main force. My role as Bennett's 'horse thief' caused alarm when I asked permission to visit a Station, and I wanted to visit all of them. Quite soon, my pleas for a hearing were accepted and eventually I was made most welcome at all Stations within the Command. I lectured on the work of the PFF, the vital need for precise timing, accurate navigation and disciplined flying. The message appealed to the best of the aircrew and soon I could ensure that only they passed through the fine mesh of the selection process.

It is sometimes assumed that it was only the 'old hands' — those who were beginning a second tour of operations — who were chosen for the PFF. This is not so. I made it my business to visit the Operational Training Units where freshman aircrew were completing their preparation for front-line service. Whenever I could, I recruited the cream of these units also. In total, I selected nearly 20,000 aircrew for the PFF, the vast majority of whom were either personally interviewed by me or who were accepted on the recommendation of officers in whose judgement I had total faith. I deeply regret that a third of those young men were lost while flying with the Pathfinder Force.

I was not always successful in getting what I wanted. As a typical example, I was beaten to the punch by Guy Gibson at the time when he was vetting crews for the new 617 Squadron. Although he did not know it then, these were the men who would fly on the Dams raid. We met at 5 Group and he warned me not to poach any of his newly selected pilots, and in particular his Flight Commanders. The creation of 617 Squadron was so secret that I thought he was talking about 106 Squadron, which he had until then been commanding. It happened that I was desperate for a Squadron Commander for 83 Squadron. I reasoned that, if the Flight Commanders were as good as Gibson was saying, then one of them would be ideal to fit that post. The pilot in question was John Searby, and I had him posted to command on the same day. Gibson was livid. He discovered that one of his prize selections — Dave Shannon — was under instruction at the PFF Training Unit at Warboys. Gibson winkled him out of Warboys at dead of night and he became one of the star performers of the Dams raid. So I didn't win them all!

Although I cannot now put a face to young Selwyn Alcock, I can draw a great deal of comparison with others like him. By the autumn of 1943, when he joined 83 Squadron, we had a rich seam of outstanding aircrew who had done very well in the early stages of Bomber Command's campaign. I could still today name many of them, but it would be unfair to do so. Like him, they were the experienced pilots whom I had recruited, who had joined a Pathfinder squadron, but who were still learning their trade as 'backers up' in the target marking techniques. His record, his swift progress, suggests that he might eventually have become a 'primary marker' or even a master bomber. As what I would call a senior apprentice, progressing through the complicated duties of pathfinding, he needed only time to gain more experience. Sadly, as with many others, his time ran out.

Alcock was fortunate to fly with several first-class PFF names at Wyton. Many of his fellow pilots were approaching the end of their Pathfinder tour which, in 1943, was in the order of sixty sorties. Their experience, and the fact that they had survived thus far, must have been a deal of comfort to freshman PFF aircrew like Alcock who were just starting their own tours. Where he was unlucky was his date of joining. It coincided with the 'Bomber' Harris dream of wrecking Berlin in tandem with the USAAF 8th Air Force. This dream was to become a nightmare for the C-in-C. The Americans did not join in his campaign because they were neither trained nor equipped to bomb by night, and any attempt by the B-17s to reach Berlin in daylight would have been a massacre. Bomber Command alone carried through the Harris plan. Our crews faced thousands of heavy radar-controlled guns and too many radar-equipped night-fighters. They took a heavy toll of our bombers during that terrible winter.

We did not realise just how good the night-fighters were at defending their Reich. We knew nothing of the 'jazz music', or 'slanting music', which caught Alcock and his crew, because so few of its victims came back to report this new tactic. In fact, it was towards the end of 1944 before we became aware of the upward firing guns which had nearly put an end to the Harris plan for destroying Berlin. Oddly enough, I was one of the very few who did survive an attack.

On 2 February 1943, I was flying a Stirling over Cologne. The bombs had been dropped and I was remaining straight and level, waiting for the photo-flash to explode. After about fifteen seconds, my bomb aimer announced that the aiming point photograph had been taken. I made a hasty turn to starboard, diving at the same time. Simultaneously, I was aware of a raking burst of cannon fire directly under the bomb bay. This burst shattered my instrument panel, destroyed the hydraulic system, wounded four of my crew, and severed the lateral controls. So, I was in a steep diving turn to starboard with the turn and dive increasing and with no means of countering a situation which was getting worse by the second.

My reflex action was to take all power off and I made a stab at pulling all throttles back. In my haste I missed the four levers and grabbed only two, those controlling the port engines. This had the immediate effect of arresting the turn and dive, and the starboard wing came up slowly.

I had gone through several thousand feet of cloud. I had no horizon and my blind flying panel was 'kaputt' but, having stopped my descent, I could regain directional control by the use of the outer engines. Rather after the fashion of a paddle-steamer skipper on the river!

The situation stabilised, I was able to climb back through the cloud only to find that the Pole Star was not where it should have been. I was heading east instead of west. The Pole Star was restored to the starboard quarter by a cautious turn and the Flight Engineer produced a rough homeward course for me to steer. I stayed on top of the cloud and only sought sanctuary when attacked once more by a fighter before we reached the coast. The bomb aimer obtained a pin-point as we crossed out, and we were more or less home and dry.

I relate this incident to illustrate how relatively simple it was for a night-fighter to approach a bomber with stealth from below, in the gunners' blind spot. I was lucky, I got away with it, but my adventure had an almost incredible sequel. Since the war, I have been several times invited to attend reunions, in Germany, of those same fighter pilots who inflicted such losses on our bomber squadrons. When you read the following pages, you will encounter one of them. His name was Willi Herget. We met, we became friends, and several times I visited his home.

On one occasion I was Willi's guest at a special banquet in Munich, lavishly funded by a German television company and at which he and several other highly decorated former Luftwaffe pilots were being lionised. Each was introduced with the usual 'oompah, oompah' of a Bavarian band, followed by an uproar of cheers and much banging of steins on table tops. When it came to Willi's turn, and having acknowledged the pandemonium, he stood on the table and spoke at length about me. To my deep embarrassment, he introduced me as a composite character embracing the combined skills of Leonard Cheshire, Guy Gibson, Johnny Fauquier and Don Bennett. He then, at length, told the assembly how he had shot me down, over Cologne, back in 1943. The news was greeted with huge acclaim. For the next few minutes, I was sure the roof must come down or the walls cave in.

Willi died some years after this excellent celebration, and happily never discovered that, after further investigation, another famous Luftwaffe ace was formally credited with the attack on my aircraft. I was just very pleased, for Willi's sake, that he could savour his moment of glory at Munich. I would have loathed for him to learn that I made it back to base that night.

Later in this book, you will read the extraordinary story of some Belgian villagers and their dedication to the memory of men whom I had selected but who did not survive the war. I am delighted that Norman Mackie was able to represent 83 Squadron at their recent remembrance ceremonies. Norman was very near to being the ideal Pathfinder. An exceptional pilot, resourceful in every way, he was Selwyn Alcock's good friend of fifty years ago and is my good friend still today. Alcock was indeed fortunate to be influenced by such a man.

I too could have piped an eye if I had been present at those ceremonies. I do this frequently when I visit the War Cemetery at Arnhem and see the young children tending the graves of the RAF aircrew and Airborne soldiers who died there. As each generation of children moves up to a higher school, so does the next crop of infants take over this simple solemn task. Long may the children of Europe and of the Commonwealth be given an awareness of that which is now past.

Wartime adversaries, peacetime friends.

'Hamish' Mahaddie, pictured in the 1950s, and Wilhelm Herget, in 1944.

v

They shall grow not old, as we that are left grow old:
Age shall not weary them, nor the years condemn.
At the going down of the sun and in the morning
We will remember them.

As the stars that shall be bright when we are dust,
Moving in marches upon the plain,
As the stars that are starry in the time of our darkness,
To the end, to the end, they remain.

from FOR THE FALLEN
by Laurence Binyon

Author's Introduction

When war erupted in 1939, I was seven years old. When it ended, in 1945, I was thirteen. The most impressionable years of my boyhood, therefore, were dominated by a passion for all things warlike. In my simple childish way, I enjoyed growing up in a world where every day brought something new and exciting, where boredom was an unknown sensation.

Even now, the images have not faded. A summer's evening, when a Company of tired, half-naked soldiers arrived in the quiet suburban street where we lived. They had come directly from the beaches of Dunkirk. Three were billeted with us for several months. Pre-war Regulars, they were the product of the orphanage and the broken home. With no family roots behind them, they treated my mother as their own. I sat at their feet and soaked up their stories of France and the life of a soldier.

The Sheffield 'blitz', and long nights in the air-raid shelter. Eight miles away, the centre of that great city was being torn apart. Sometimes, the grown-ups let me peek at the sky to watch the bursting shells and racing tracer. Eventual sleep, and my father carrying his drowsy child back to the house in the soft light of dawn.

Like every local gang of lads in Great Britain, we formed our private army. Bits of discarded webbing, tin hats from the Great War, broomsticks fashioned into rifles and machine guns, we equipped ourselves as infantry and went to war against the armies of the neighbouring streets. And when we were resting between campaigns, we searched the gutters and gardens for shrapnel and bits of bomb. Collections of shattered metal cluttered our bedrooms and drove our mothers to mutiny.

I kept a scrap-book, carefully snipping from censored newspapers the latest reports of the Western Desert, of Normandy, and of the war at sea. Above all, I consumed every word published on the Royal Air Force. 'Plane spotting' was a compulsion. I knew the Whitley from the Wellington, the Lancaster from the Halifax, the Spitfire Mark V from the Spitfire Mark XII. Like my pals, I could detect the distant song of the Merlin and know that it was not a Daimler Benz.

Rotherham, our home town in those years, lay under the route of the bombers when they left their Yorkshire lairs and began the four hours' haul to Germany. As the sun set at the end of those golden summer days, every family went into the garden and, heads thrown back, watched the hundreds of four-engined 'heavies' coming together to form their miles-long stream. A neighbour had lost her son in a 'plane like these. 'Go on, boys, give 'em Hell', she would shout as the sinister horde roared and strained for altitude.

Although we did not know it at the time, the very special 617 Squadron was getting ready to attack the great dams of Western Germany. To gain practice in ultra-low flying over still water, they flew often over the reservoirs of Derbyshire, not so far from Rotherham. There was the day when the sound of multiple engines propelled me into the garden in time to duck as one of 617's Lancs passed over the house at a height of no more than fifty feet. Who was it? Guy Gibson? Mickey Martin? Dave Shannon? Which of my boyhood heroes rattled our chimney-pots that afternoon? I shall never know.

Then there was the time, an early morning, when an even louder thunder of engines sent me racing from the breakfast table to the back door in time to see nine Lancasters crossing over at a thousand feet or less. Never before, or later, did I see these big bombers flying in tight formation. In perfect geometry with each other, they flew in three 'vics' of three. Two had a stopped engine and a feathered propeller. Another had a dog-eared hole in the wingtip. The leader of the leading 'vic', his bomb doors hanging open wide, trailed a dense plume of oily smoke, a fire still burning within the fuselage. Who were these crews, from what raid were they returning? In my imagination then, and still today, this was 'the boss' — a commanding officer — being brought home by his squadron pilots.

I have failed, in adulthood, to pin-point that moment, to discover which long-vanished flight swept over Yorkshire with an invincibility and pride which, even now, causes me to miss a beat. What manner of men were these who, finding a comrade in trouble, escorted him back to base as though on a Royal review?

In later years I became a writer. My topics were the Navy, the Marines, soldiers and long-forgotten military campaigns, but never the bombers. So many other authors, experts in their field, had written so many fine books on the subject that there seemed no space on the shelves for yet another contribution.

All of that changed a couple of years ago. By chance, I became involved in the story of a man named Selwyn Alcock. Just one of thousands, he had been a pilot. He had flown with Bomber Command. He was, possibly, one of those whom I had watched, cocooned within their steel and aluminium machines, as they passed over our home those summer evenings nearly half a century before. Some were, or became, household names. Their courage, their leadership and flying skills, caught the public imagination. These were the exceptions, the chosen few. The majority were, and remained, unlauded and unknown. Those who failed to return rest now under the North Sea or under silent rows of stone in every country of North West Europe. The survivors, after the war, accepted gratefully, and perhaps with surprise, the prospect of leading normal lives and of achieving obscure old age.

Selwyn Alcock was simply 'one of the bomber boys'. He never knew fame or glory, never aspired to influential rank. In January of 1944 he disappeared into the fiery cauldron known to history as the Battle of Berlin. With the passing years, most of the people who had known him and loved him completed their earthly span. Their memories of this pleasant young man died with them. Apart from some medals and a handful of fading photographs, there was little evidence that he had ever existed. By 1990, when I promised Dorothy that I would try to search out what had happened to her first husband, the trail had become cold. Even to discover which schools he had attended, what interests he had or beliefs he held, was to make an uneasy journey back into a world which no longer exists.

Gradually, as the pieces of the jigsaw fell into place, I came to understand that Selwyn Alcock represented an entire generation of young men who fly no more. That fact alone seemed to justify the compilation of some form of written record. Then, in 1991, a chance meeting in Belgium revealed a totally unexpected ending to his story. In seeking to reconstruct the life and times of an unsung bomber pilot, I encountered an act of humanity which moved me greatly. The motive for writing this book then became overwhelming. It is my personal tribute to Selwyn, to his long-ago comrades, and to the people of Sautour. Even more importantly, the book is intended to give the families of all former aircrew some understanding of the way they lived and the way they fought their war.

Roger Perkins
Newton Abbot
Devon

1992

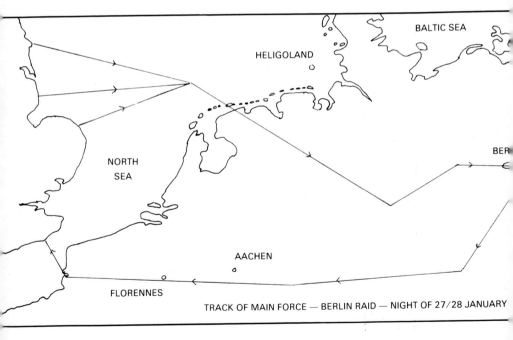

BALTIC SEA

HELIGOLAND

NORTH
SEA

BER

AACHEN

FLORENNES

TRACK OF MAIN FORCE — BERLIN RAID — NIGHT OF 27/28 JANUARY

The Hunters

Paulin Mathot was just twenty years of age. He had been living in the woods for many weeks. Like thousands of other young Belgians, he knew that sooner or later he would receive instructions from the occupying power to report for enforced labour in Germany. To escape that certainty, he had left his parents' home in Phillipeville and taken refuge in the thinly populated countryside around Sautour, six miles to the south.

The night of 27 January 1944 was still and frosty. Paulin trod cautiously through the deserted copses and fields, scavenging for food. Thin clouds partly obscured the glittering stars. The moon had not yet risen. The only sound was that of an occasional aircraft taking off from the Luftwaffe night-fighter base at Florennes, a few miles to the north.

Shortly after eleven o'clock, the sky began to sound with the familiar throb of Rolls Royce Merlin engines. Paulin had heard it many times before when Bomber Command had chosen to direct its squadrons across this area. Now five hundred Lancasters were moving steadily across Luxembourg and Southern Belgium, heading home to England. They formed an invisible stream, ten miles wide, sixty miles long, and four miles above the earth. Three hours earlier they had unloaded more than two thousand tons of explosive and incendiary bombs on the city of Berlin. Five hundred and sixty-seven civilians had been killed, twenty thousand made homeless, fifty industrial premises damaged, and the life of the city even further disrupted. The raid was one of nineteen major night-time attacks launched against Germany's capital during that autumn and bitter winter. Thirty-four Lancasters were to be lost this night. More than two hundred young airmen would not see the dawn.

Paulin Mathot was not the only hunter on the prowl. While he hoped to snare a rabbit or snatch a sleeping pheasant, there were others who sought much bigger prey. One of these was Major Wilhelm Herget. At thirty-three, with almost four years of combat flying behind him, he was one of Germany's most highly decorated night-fighter pilots. He had taken off from Florennes an hour earlier when reports made it clear that the British had left Berlin by a southerly route. Flying with him in his twin-engined Messerschmitt Bf 110 were his navigator and radar operator, Hans Liebherr, and his gunner, Emil Gröss. Together they had already destroyed many 'Tommies', the big Royal Air Force four-engined bombers which were systematically laying waste the major cities of their homeland. In one such raid, Herget's wife had been killed. He and his crew, aided by their SN-2 radar and additional radar from the ground, were a deadly threat to any bomber crew unlucky enough to come within their range. Now, having climbed steadily through the darkness to 20,000 feet, Herget was carefully inserting himself into the unseen stream of Lancasters. His attention was fixed entirely upon his instrument panel and the information he was receiving through his headphones from his ground controllers. Only the occasional buffeting of his aircraft, when it passed through the

1

decaying turbulence caused by a bomber's propellers, confirmed that there were other aircraft around him.

That he was at the right height and on the correct heading was confirmed by Hans Liebherr. His radar screen was showing several 'blips', each of which represented a potential target. Slowly, with the patience of long practice, Liebherr directed his pilot to bring the Bf 110 into an attacking position behind and slightly below one of these 'blips'. It was pointless to hurry. The 'Tommy' would be most probably unaware of his approach. The enemy pilot was flying straight and level and was not using his rear-looking 'Monica' radar. His gunners would be constantly scanning the black void, but they would see nothing as long as Herget kept low. That way the shape of his aircraft would not be outlined by the stars.

For several minutes Herget edged towards an attacking position. Only the smallest movements of the controls were required to adjust his speed and course so that they matched precisely those of the bomber. He wanted to get close before opening fire. For *experten* like him, it was a matter of professional pride to make a 'kill' with a minimum expenditure of ammunition.

Herget's official report of the encounter has not survived the years. The events of the next few moments can be described only on the basis of probability and the evidence of other such attacks when there were survivors who could tell the tale.

Liebherr announced his latest speed and distance calculations. This was the critical phase of the attack because his SN-2 radar could not function at ranges of less than 500 metres. If the 'Tommy' pilot chose at this stage to make a turn or change altitude, Liebherr would need to make a fresh search and commence a new attack.

For the first time since he had lifted off from Florennes, Major Herget raised his head and looked out through the canopy. He no longer needed to depend upon Liebherr. There, 500 metres ahead and 100 metres above, he saw the dull red glow of engine exhausts. Fractionally opening the throttles, he crept towards the barely visible source of light. A minute later, cat-like, the Bf 110 slid under the bomber's huge black bulk. Herget recognised the distinctive shape of a Lancaster. No more than sixty metres separated the two aircraft.

The German had two alternative means of attack. Ahead of him, in the nose of his aircraft, he had four 20mm and 30mm cannon, aimed to fire directly forwards. Behind, in the rear cockpit area, he had two more 20mm cannon. These were mounted obliquely, at an angle of 70 degrees, so that they pointed upwards and forwards. These were code-named *schrage musik*, or 'jazz music', and were a secret which British intelligence did not detect until much later in the war.

The weapon was brutally simple, and fatal to its victims. Flying behind and beneath the target, the German pilot could make his attack in relative safety. His own aircraft was hidden in the blackness of the ground, far below. British heavy bombers were not fitted with a ventral turret, so their crews could not keep downward observation.

The usual aiming point was the area of wing between the engines which held much of the bomber's fuel. A short burst of gunfire was enough to rupture the tanks, set alight to the petrol, and create a fierce 'blow-torch' which devoured the internal structure of the wing. The attacking pilot would then pull away to one side and watch as the stricken bomber, engulfed in flames, entered its final dive. Within a short while, the wing lost its strength and broke off. If the crew had not already taken to their parachutes, they would be trapped by centrifugal force within the rapidly spinning fuselage.

Herget did not, on this night, follow the standard pattern of attack. His victim was outward bound, much of its fuel already expended. The wing tanks contained only petrol vapour, itself an explosive mixture which could endanger his own aircraft. He decided to fire directly upwards into the bomber's fuselage. It no longer carried a lethal bomb-load which his gun-fire might detonate. It offered no threat to him.

Staring upwards through the gun-sight fixed in his cockpit roof, he aimed at the target's nose and pressed the firing button. The stream of cannon shells punched fatally back along the Lancaster's belly. Three seconds were enough for his task.

The bomber did not burn, it did not even change course, but already it was a dying aircraft. The 20mm shells did not simply puncture the aluminium skin. They had exploded inside the fuselage, sending splinters of steel in every direction. Men had been killed or injured, equipment destroyed and, it seems likely, the flying controls damaged.

Paul Mathot stood gazing at the sky. He heard the sound of gunfire, away to the east, but it was impossible to judge at what distance. Four minutes passed and then he saw a glimmer of light over Frimont Wood. Something was falling out of the sky and it was coming towards Sautour. He heard the sound of tearing metal and of engines screaming at a level far higher than normal. Following the shape as it passed over him, he saw that it was a large aircraft. It was spinning down and breaking apart. A moment later came a series of thumping noises as twenty-two tons of wreckage hit the ground.

The young Belgian made his way through the fields and began to search for possible survivors. During the next few hours he discovered that there were none. Shortly after dawn he found a body beside a track running through Frimont Wood. The dead man lay amongst a scattering of wreckage, his Sidcot flying suit blackened by fire. This was the bomber's centre section and the body was that of the mid-upper gunner.

Also searching through the woods was another local man, Michel Putzeys. Of the same age as Paulin Mathot, he had already completed a year of enforced labour in Germany but had been sent back to Sautour because of his skills as a charcoal burner. Charcoal was needed by German industry, so Michel had authority to erect a shed in the woods and to work there. At first light, he too found a body. Laid outstretched on its back, it was that of a blue-eyed man with blond hair. He was wearing an unopened parachute pack. This was the bomber's wireless operator. He had been thrown out of the aircraft when it broke apart over the village.

Half a mile away, in a small valley, was the house of the Jacques family. Like Paulin Mathot and Michel Putzeys, the menfolk of this family were small-holders and foresters. An hour after retiring for the night, they were awakened by a violent noise. Rushing outside, they found the tail section and gun turret of a bomber. It lay in a field, fifty metres from the house. Across the road, opposite their front door and beside the small concrete structure which bridged a narrow stream, was the body of an airman. A dark-haired, powerfully built man, he seemed to have been thrown clear of the wreckage and was therefore the bomber's rear gunner. With his father and brothers, the ten years-old Désiré Jacques searched through the wreckage and the clothing of the dead man to remove any items which might be of value to the Resistance movement or to any Allied airman attempting to evade capture.

Having shed its rear and centre section, the Lancaster had plunged over the tightly packed buildings of the village and smashed into a field little more than a hundred metres from the nearest house. As it dropped, small pieces of airframe broke away to fall as metallic rain in nearby rooftops. One larger piece, a complete wingtip, spun down and crashed against the rear wall of the house which was, and still is, the home of the Wilmot family. Young Franz Wilmot and his father tried to lift it away from the building, but found it too heavy.

Paulin Mathot left Frimont Wood and walked down into the village. With his friends, he went to the shallow crater where the major part of the aircraft lay. Intact and upright, it consisted of the cabin section and the main wings, or main spar, with the four engines still in place. Climbing cautiously inside, he saw the superficially uninjured bodies of four men. Two were wearing parachute packs. Two other packs were still in their stowage racks. It was evident that he was looking at the remains of the pilot, bomb aimer, flight engineer and navigator.

With other villagers, Paulin began to remove anything which could be more useful to him than to the Germans. In severely rationed Belgium, there was an immediate interest in cigarettes, chocolate, wrist-watches, medical equipment and protective clothing. The parachutes were quickly taken away and hidden. Later they were turned into dress material and underwear for the womenfolk. Pieces of perspex from the smashed canopy were utilised to make crucifixes and other items of personal jewellery. Panels of aluminium were taken to be made into household items such as cooking utensils and even door keys.

In a field near his home, Michel Putzeys found the bomber's radio set. Most of the valves were broken, but it was smuggled away and handed over to the local

4

Resistance movement so that they might salvage some of the parts. Other items retrieved from the surrounding area were the inflatable dinghy and a Verey pistol.

By nine-thirty it was evident that German search parties were making their way down the road to Sautour from their radar station at nearby Les Mignelotte. A small aircraft, a Fieseler Storch, started to make low sweeps over the locality. Paulin Mathot had no wish to be caught in the cordon which the Germans were placing around the village. He made off, back into the sanctuary of the woods.

Luftwaffe salvage crews removed the larger pieces of wreckage during the following three days. The dead airmen were taken away in a manner which the villagers judged to be decent and correct. As one of them described it, 'with piety'. They were buried in individual graves at Jusaine Rosée, a hamlet on the fringe of Florennes airfield. Several Luftwaffe officers are thought to have attended the service which was conducted by a local Roman Catholic priest.

For Wilhelm Herget, the night's events amounted to nothing more than yet another victory. This Lancaster was only one of forty-four heavy bombers which he was to shoot down by night before the end of the war. He would soon forget it. For the families of the Lancaster's crew, however, it would be a different story.

The Beginning of a Quest

Earlier on the day of the crash, 27 January 1944, a document had arrived on the desk of Air Vice Marshal Donald Bennett, Air Officer Commanding the Royal Air Force's Pathfinder Force (No 8 Group). It was a recommendation for the award of a Distinguished Flying Cross to a pilot serving with 83 Squadron, based at Wyton, Huntingdonshire. Having scanned the wording, Bennett counter-signed the paper with a conventional 'Strongly recommended'. There was nothing exceptional here. Nearly twenty-two thousand DFCs were awarded between 1939 and 1945. This was one of the 'non-immediate' awards which recognised consistent good work over a long period of time rather than a single exceptional act of gallantry. Compiled by the Officer Commanding 83 Squadron, it read:

Flight Lieutenant Alcock, as Captain of a heavy bomber, has completed 46 operational flights against the enemy, 15 of these being with the Path Finder Force. Throughout his operational tour he has been detailed to attack most of the heavily defended targets in Germany, including 7 sorties in the Battle of Berlin. Without fail, Flight Lieutenant Alcock has carried out his arduous duties with determination and skill, always courageously pressing home his attack to his utmost. On two recent occasions, when approaching Berlin, his aircraft suffered very concentrated and accurate anti-aircraft fire which resulted in an engine being put out of action on each occasion. Despite this, Flight Lieutenant Alcock continued on his bombing runs and marked and attacked his target successfully. His exemplary operational conduct and valour have contributed largely to the

*success of the operations in which he has taken part. I strongly recommend the
award of the Distinguished Flying Cross.*

Selwyn Alcock was the pilot of the Lancaster brought down by Wilhelm Herget.
The trip to Berlin, his last, was his forty-ninth operational sortie. He died without
knowing that his previous services had, at last, been officially recognised. The
award did not appear in the London Gazette until 13 October 1944.

Forty-six years later, the medal passed into the hands of a private collector, the
author of this book. Alcock's surviving next-of-kin parted with it on the understanding that her many unanswered questions, regarding the circumstances of her
first husband's death, would be investigated. The following pages are a summary
of the chance encounters and new friendships which resulted from those researches.

First Tour

Selwyn Henry Alcock was born in Edgbaston, Birmingham, on 16 February 1919,
the only son of William George and Eva May Alcock. The family settled in Brierley
Hill, Worcestershire, where Selwyn's father was Vicar of St John the Evangelist, in
the Parish of Brockmoor. The boy is still remembered there, by elderly villagers, as
being unusually obedient and respectful, with a gentle and open personality.

He attended, until 1927, St Luke's Church of England School, Blankenhall,
Wolverhampton. Showing promise as a chorister, he moved to Worcester Cathedral School for two years and then, in 1930, transferred on a musical scholarship to
Wells Cathedral School, in Somerset. His fine voice was to feature in the Cathedral
choir for the next six years.

A growing interest in sport was encouraged by his teachers. An all-rounder,
he became the school's Captain of Rugby in 1935 and Captain of Hockey in 1936,
his final year.

He had decided, no doubt with his father's support, to train for a career in the
Anglican Church. Leaving Wells, he moved to Knutsford Ordination Test School,
near Chester, for a year and a half. Then, at the age of nineteen, he went up to
Durham University to commence a three-years degree course at St John's College.
He made an instant impact upon the sporting scene by stroking the College eight,
gaining his Colours in rugby and hockey, and playing cricket for the University. It
was a golden freshman year, but the promise of greater things to come was denied
by the events of September 1939.

As soon as war was declared, Selwyn volunteered for service with the RAF.
He abandoned his studies at Durham but, to his disappointment, the Air Ministry
did not immediately accept his offer. To pass the time, he took a job in the laboratory
of Guy's Hospital, London, and then at a glass works near his home town.

Full circle. Three eyewitnesses to the crash, Michel Putzeys, Paulin Mathot and Franz Wilmot, examine a recently recovered length of fuel pipe from the doomed Lancaster. Back in England, the author unites it with the medals which first prompted the investigation.

The call to arms came in the Spring of 1940. On 9 March, he enlisted as 955422, Aircraftsman 2nd Class. Nine months later, in November, he completed all his initial ground and elementary flying training, received his 'wings', and was granted a Commission as a Pilot Officer 'on probation in the General Duties Branch of the Royal Air Force Volunteer Reserve'.

It was during that fateful summer of 1940 that Selwyn met the girl who, two years later, he was to marry. With hundreds of other young aspiring airmen, he had been sent to Torquay, in South Devon, to No 13 Initial Training Wing. The town's largest hotels had been requisitioned by the Air Ministry as temporary accommodation for the trainees. A chance encounter with a local girl, Dorothy Gilbert, led to romance. As she describes him: 'He was very handsome, about five feet ten, with dark wavy hair. It was love at first sight for both of us'. Dorothy moved north, settled in with Selwyn's parents at the Vicarage, and took a job in a local factory.

Having gained his pilot's brevet, Selwyn was posted for eight weeks to No 2 School of Air Navigation at RAF Cranage, Cheshire. Here he learned the techniques of aerial navigation on the twin-engined Anson. The next step was No 14 Operational Training Unit where he was taught to fly the Hampden, and the skills of navigation, gunnery and bombing in this type of aircraft. A twin-engined bomber, with a crew of four, it cruised at 140 miles per hour at 12,000 feet with a bomb load of 2000 pounds. The load could be increased to 4500 pounds, but this reduced by half the maximum operational radius of 840 miles. Defence was provided by twin .303 Vickers machine guns in dorsal and ventral turrets, one fixed forward-firing Browning machine gun operated by the pilot, and a single Vickers, in the nose, which could be operated if necessary by the navigator.

When the Hampden made its first daylight sorties, early in the war, German fighter pilots found that they could shoot it down at their leisure by attacking from slightly ahead of the beam, or from ahead and above, approaches not covered by the helpless Hampden's guns. Daylight sorties were abandoned after severe losses. When Selwyn received his first operational posting, on 13 May 1941, the Hampden was employed exclusively on night raids. He joined 83 Squadron at RAF Scampton, in Lincolnshire.

His first flight into enemy airspace came on 25 May 1941. He flew as navigator to Flight Lieutenant Tony Mills DFC in Hampden X3144. The plan was to drop a mine in the waters off the French port of Brest. Bad weather and poor visibility prevented Selwyn from fixing the ordered dropping point, so the mine was brought back to Scampton.

His second trip, again as navigator to Tony Mills, took him back to Brest, this time for a bombing raid. The major German warships *Scharnhorst, Prinz Eugen* and *Gneisenau* had taken refuge in the port after forays into the North Atlantic. Bomber Command was attempting to sink or at least damage them. A mixed force of one hundred and four Hampdens, Whitleys and Wellingtons went on the raid, and all returned safely. Some port installations were wrecked, but there were no hits on the ships. Nine months later they broke out of Brest and escaped to Germany.

He made ten more operational flights during the following weeks, all of them as navigator to Tony Mills. Like all newly qualified pilots, Selwyn was required to gain experience before being entrusted with a crew of his own. He did not become a 'captain of aircraft' until 15 September when he flew X3601 on a comparatively easy raid against the docks at Le Havre. Thereafter, he took part in most of 83 Squadron's raids through to December 1941 when he was posted to 49 Squadron (the other Hampden unit sharing the facilities at Scampton). He completed his first tour of thirty operations with 49 Squadron in April 1942.

The sorties were all restricted by the Hampden's short range. They were directed at military and economic targets in Hamburg, Kiel, Huls, Aachen, Osnabrück, and other German towns, and sea mines were dropped off the coasts of Brittany and Holland, but the results barely justified the effort. On 22 October 1941, for example, when 123 crews were ordered to attack industrial buildings in Mannheim, less than half claimed to have found the target. One house was destroyed, thirty-five damaged, six people killed, and one injured. On the other side of the balance sheet, the RAF lost four aircraft and the lives of nineteen highly trained aircrew.

Finding the Way

The story of Selwyn Alcock's operational career, between 1941 and 1944, is in microcosm the story of Bomber Command's long and costly struggle to dominate the night skies of Europe. The problems were overcome only in the last year of the war, by which time he and thousands of other aircrew were already dead. Their sacrifice was, at least in part, the consequence of two decades of official neglect, between the wars, of Great Britain's aviation capability.

Although the authorities, in the late 1930s, had made a belated and panicky attempt to encourage the development of new aircraft and weaponry, the British, like the Germans, viewed the multi-engined types as being useful mainly for troop transport, maritime reconnaissance, tactical bombing in support of ground forces, and pin-point daylight attacks on military targets at ranges of no more than a few hundred miles. Only in America was the concept of long-range strategic bombing starting to receive serious consideration. The result was that the RAF entered the war with a light bomber, the Blenheim, and three medium types, the Whitley, Hampden and Wellington. Of these, only the Wellington would later stand the test of prolonged operations, and then exclusively under cover of darkness.

Airframe and engine design were not the only areas of deficiency. The standard RAF bomb was the 250 pounder. Its destructive power was modest, having a quarter of the explosive contained in the RAF's heaviest bombs of 1918 vintage. Air Marshal Sir Arthur Harris, later to become Commander in Chief of

Bomber Command, dismissed it as 'a ridiculous missile'. By 1945, the weight of the largest bomb in his armoury would have grown to ten tons, but that was still more than three years into the future.

For their own defence, aircrew depended upon machine guns which fired the .303 rifle bullet familiar to every infantryman who had fought in the Great War of 1914-1918. Advances had been made with tracer and incendiary rounds, but the bomber's firepower was puny compared with that of the Luftwaffe's new fighters. This weakness was never resolved. To have equipped the bombers with guns of heavier calibre and greater range would have added to their weight, thereby reducing the bomb load. This was a compromise which Harris consistently rejected, even when the loss rate became so severe that the continuing existence of his Command was called into question.

By far the greatest problem, however, was navigation. At the time of Selwyn's entry into the bombing business, British scientists were working hard to develop radar equipment which was smaller and lighter, but much of their effort was directed at assisting the Royal Navy and Coastal Command in the U-boat war. Primitive airborne sets had been fitted, with negligible success, to some Blenheims during the Battle of Britain, but Bomber Command would not receive navigation radar until 1943. Its aircrew, therefore, were restricted to traditional means of finding their way around Europe's dangerous night skies. This meant little more than looking at the map on those few occasions when the ground could be seen, and calculating a position by 'dead reckoning'. This theoretical exercise was based upon time and distance flown, with an allowance for the strength and direction of the wind. It was the task of the Staff Meteorological Officers to forecast the winds which a crew might encounter at various stages of its planned flight, but these officers had no access to weather reports from the Continent. As a consequence, their forecasts were often wildly inaccurate.

Navigators were given basic instruction in astro-navigation, but this was never a popular activity. As a pilot of that period described it: "The navigator needed to clamber back behind the pilot, remove a hatch, 'shoot' his chosen star through the small opening, try to hold steady while the aircraft bucketed around the sky, then climb quickly back to his station and do his sums. Operating the sextant meant removing the gloves, and this invariably led to frozen fingers. It was an exhausting experience, and rarely produced an accurate fix."

When it is realised that a bomber's crew was often contending with temperatures of minus 40 degrees Centigrade inside a fuselage which was constantly being tossed around by turbulence, it is not surprising that the RAF's early bombing campaign achieved so little. Thick cloud, dense ground haze in the industrial areas, lack of technical equipment, inaccurate wind readings, heavy icing on wings and propellers, they all combined to lead pilots and navigators astray. Crews frequently got lost and dropped their bombs five, fifty or a hundred miles from their designated targets. Selwyn flew his first tour with Bomber Command at a time

83 Sqn at war, March 1941. This Hampden crew, photographed at RAF Scampton, consisted of (left to right): Unknown, F/O J M Bousfield DFC, P/O Haggerty, S/L N W Timmerman DFC and F/O N S Royle DFC. All survived their first tour, but Norman Royle died a year later in a training accident, and Jack Bousfield was killed in February 1943 while serving with 50 Sqn.

The 83 Sqn crest originated on the Western Front in 1918. Equipped with two-seater 'spotter' aircraft, the FE2b, the Squadron was employed on reconnaissance duties around Bapaume and Cambrai. On the night of 4 June, GHQ asked for a 'recce' flight to be made over suspected German positions. Three aircraft flew through very bad weather to obtain the needed information. The pilots and observers were each awarded a DFC for their feat, and it was later commemorated by the six points on the antler motif.

11

when it lacked the capability to perform the task expected of it.

The last sortie of that tour was flown on 10 April 1942. It was his thirtieth and, like most of the others, it was blighted by adverse weather. The target was the Krupp industrial complex at Essen. He claimed in his report to have found the city, but it is unlikely that he did so. Post-war investigation showed that, of 172 crews which reported a successful attack, only six had actually hit the city. Twelve houses were knocked down and seven people were killed. Krupp was untouched. For its part, the RAF lost sixteen aircraft that night, seventy aircrew were 'missing in action'. Ice, engine failures, and the Ruhr's dense 'flak' (anti-aircraft artillery) defences, all took their toll.

A Fresh Start

It was time for a change. Selwyn went home on leave to Brockmoor. He had been promoted to Flying Officer and, although he had no ribbons on his chest, he was the hero of the village. The parishioners had kept track of his movements and they cheered whenever, during a daylight training or test flight, he made low passes over the Vicarage.

In June 1942, having qualified as an Instructor at RAF Upavon, he was posted to No 24 OTU (Operational Training Unit) at RAF Honeybourne, near Evesham. It was not far from his home and he would be there for the next fifteen months, teaching new pilots how to fly Whitleys and Wellingtons. The time was right to get married. His father conducted the ceremony at St John's, Brockmoor, on 10 October 1942. Dorothy, always called 'Betty' by her in-laws, became Mrs Alcock. Selwyn had lost interest in the Church as a future career and was looking for wider horizons. Perhaps, if the war ended soon, he and his bride could have a place of their own and start a family.

The war did not end soon. In September 1943, having completed his time at Honeybourne and having learned to fly Lancasters, he was posted back to 83 Squadron. His old unit had moved from Scampton to Wyton, in Huntingdonshire. The Hampdens had been long since consigned to training units or the scrapyard. In their place, the Squadron had the Lancaster Mark I. Although still not at that stage a complete answer to Bomber Command's requirements, it was a vast improvement on the twin-engined types of 1940. Its wing span of 102 feet supported an all-up weight of 27 tons when fully loaded, or more in special circumstances. The long bomb-bay accommodated a combination of incendiaries, deep penetration and surface blast bombs with a total weight of five tons (more or less, according to the target). The seven-man crew had the benefit of heating and de-icing equipment previously unknown in service aircraft. To overcome the earlier navigational and target-finding problems, airborne radar was at last starting to reach the front-line squadrons.

*Selwyn Alcock as a chorister at
Wells Cathedral School, 1932,
and as the bridegroom at Brockmoor,
10 October 1942. His death,
fifteen months after the wedding,
had a devastating impact
upon Dorothy and his adoring parents.*

Conforming with the policy agreed by the Allied leaders at the Casablanca Conference, 'Bomber' Harris was committed to bombing Germany's major areas of population. The earlier attempts to hit specifically military and industrial targets, without causing civilian casualties, had been abandoned as technically impossible for the night bomber. The new strategy was the total destruction of entire cities. Those chosen for attack were cities having within their boundaries the industries vital to Germany's war effort and the skilled workforces needed to run them. The first city to feel the full impact of Harris's new campaign was Hamburg. It had been incinerated in July, shortly before Selwyn returned to 83 Squadron. Forty thousand people had been killed and a million more had fled in terror. The Germans had sown the wind, now they were reaping the whirlwind.

The dramatic increase in Bomber Command's destructive power was not simply the consequence of having larger aircraft with heavier bomb loads. The entire organisation had been restructured under Harris's vigorous leadership. Pilots no longer chose their own take-off times and routes, as had been the case in the early days. They no longer relied upon their own individual efforts to find the target. Now they were being marshalled over the North Sea and sent along a specified track so that they could all reach their destination as a unified striking force. With several hundred aircraft dropping their bombs within a short span of time, the ground defences and fire-fighting services were often overwhelmed. In 1943, a full Bomber Command attack brought 3000 tons of bombs onto a target in the space of thirty minutes. By 1945 that blow would be delivered in less than ten minutes.

Accuracy of bombing was still frequently wayward, but the Pathfinder Force was making rapid progress in putting matters right. Formed by Group Captain Donald Bennett in July 1942, the Pathfinders were an elite group of squadrons whose role it was to lead the attack, to be the first over the target, and to mark it with various types of pyrotechnic which, if all went well, could be clearly seen by the following main force. The old problem of finding an aiming point had been largely solved.

The initial strength of the Pathfinder Force was five squadrons. One of these was 83 Squadron, and it was the only one equipped with Lancasters. When Selwyn rejoined, in September 1943, many of these aircraft had been flying operationally for more than a year. Some had been damaged and repaired several times, others had engines and airframes which were reaching the end of their front-line lives. The wear and tear was such that few aircraft completed more than 150 flying hours before being lost, scrapped, or relegated to a training unit. Despite its 'serviceability' difficulties, the Squadron was in good spirits and Selwyn was glad to be back amongst those of his old friends who were still alive.

He was bringing some new friends with him. When he arrived at RAF Wyton on 10 September 1943 he arrived with the nucleus of a crew. They were an Australian, Flying Officer Bill Hewson, and an Englishman, Flight Lieutenant Eric

Sargent. Bill would be Selwyn's rear gunner, Eric his navigator. Like Selwyn, both were beginning their second tour of operations.

Second Tour

According to his contemporaries, Selwyn was an 'average' pilot. He was steady and reliable rather than naturally gifted. His personality since childhood displayed the characteristics of conformity. He lived 'by the book', and he flew by the book. He was also unusually strong. The combination of a calm temperament and great physical strength made him an ideal heavy bomber pilot. He had survived his first thirty operational sorties and had always brought his crew home intact. He had survived fifteen months as an instructor without permitting any of his pupils to get themselves into fatal situations. Now he was embarking on a second tour with the sure knowledge that, no matter how careful he might be, his prospects of seeing it through were very limited. It was a question of statistical probability. Four out of five aircrew failed to survive their first tour, only one in thirty lived long enough to complete a second. Some men went on for a third. The 'grim reaper' was waiting for all of them, every time they flew.

Despite his experience, he was treated initially by 83 Squadron as 'one of the new boys'. He needed to learn the new target marking techniques at first hand. Much had changed in the tactics of aerial warfare over Germany since his last visit. To catch up with these developments, he was sent as 'second dickey', or passenger, on two introductory sorties with other pilots.

The first came on 22 September when he accompanied Pilot Officer R King in OL-T ED601. The target was Hannover. King's job was to assist in marking the aiming point with cascades of red indicators. Apart from these two containers, his load consisted of five 1000 pounder medium capacity bombs and one 4000 pounder high capacity bomb, best known as a 'Cookie'. A long cylinder made from thin steel plate, resembling a steam boiler, its weight was almost entirely explosive. It had no aerodynamic properties. When released, it tumbled through the air with no great accuracy. Impacting the ground, it sent out a shock wave which blew nearby buildings apart. Journalists labelled it 'the blockbuster'. King's load was typical of those which Selwyn's own aircraft would be carrying when, later in the winter, he was awarded Pathfinder status.

On the following night, 23 September, he made another 'second dickey' trip, this time to Mannheim with Flight Lieutenant M R Chick in OL-S JB967. He was then declared ready to start operating as a captain of aircraft. His next problem, therefore, was to form a crew.

Bill Hewson and Eric Sargent had made their own introductory operational flights with the Squadron, flying with other pilots, and were now ready to join Selwyn. The position of the wireless operator was filled by Flight Sergeant M A

Coles, a steady NCO who flew with him until January when his place was taken by Flight Lieutenant L G Davis.

As bomb aimer, Selwyn was assigned Flight Sergeant H C Highet, but this NCO was sometimes replaced by others who came and went. It may be that Highet had a succession of head colds which prevented him from flying on a regular basis. His final replacement was Flying Officer R H Adamson who will be mentioned again later.

The key post of Flight Engineer was filled by Flight Sergeant F E Burton-Burgess. Selwyn was exceptionally lucky to have this man with him on his first three Lancaster sorties. Burton-Burgess was another 'second-tour' man, having previously served as engineer to one of 83 Squadron's most famous officers, Guy Gibson. Unfortunately he was soon replaced by a succession of others. Almost incredibly, Selwyn had eleven different flight engineers before losing his life in January. Burton-Burgess had an even shorter time to live.

Selwyn's first independent command, piloting his own aircraft, came on 10 November when, with 312 other Lancaster crews, he dropped eight 1000 pounders on the railway marshalling yards at Modane, on the French-Italian border. Visibility was excellent. Shortly after one o'clock in the morning he approached the Alps and identified the target by eye. There was no cloud, little flak, and no fighter opposition. He would never again have such an easy trip. All attacking aircraft returned safely to their bases.

A week later the Squadron went back to Mannheim. Again he flew OL-N JB309. This was a brand new Lancaster Mark III, built by A V Roe & Company, of Heathfield, Manchester. The Mark III was being produced at the rate of nearly 170 new aircraft per month and it was quickly replacing the Mark I with which 83 Squadron had been operating during the summer.

On 22 November he took the same aircraft and crew to Berlin. They very nearly did not return home. Bomber Command had been preparing for a long time to launch a sustained attack on the German capital. There had been three raids on it in August and early September, but Harris's intention now was to flatten the city and thereby force Hitler to capitulate. Harris calculated that the battle would last four months and that it would cost his command five hundred aircraft. He was almost correct in the estimate of losses, but not in his hopes for a speedy end to the war. Enormous damage was indeed inflicted on this night and on some later raids, but Berlin was too large and too dispersed for it to suffer the same 'fire storm' fate as Hamburg. To the RAF aircrew, it was 'the big city'. Its streets, factories, commercial areas, marshalling yards and open parklands covered an area forty miles in diameter.

By late 1943, the skies over Germany had become immeasurably more dangerous than when Selwyn was piloting Hampdens. The searchlight and flak batteries, especially around Berlin and the Ruhr, were numerous and efficient. All

Selwyn Alcock, newly commissioned, January 1940. Four years later he became one of the sad statistics of 83 (Pathfinder) Sqn – 879 aircrew killed, 11 ground crew died in accidents, burials at 150 sites in 14 different countries. Those who vanished without trace – 173 having no known grave – are commemorated at Runnymede.

were controlled by a sophisticated radar network which was not easily deceived by British counter-measures.

Selwyn was approaching the aiming point when his aircraft was bracketed by a salvo of radar-predicted flak. Shells exploded all around him. The fuselage was riddled and the starboard outer engine burst into flames. He pressed on with the attack so that Flight Sergeant Highet could release his bombs as planned, but it was a frightening experience. The fire was extinguished and they headed for home on three engines. The starboard outer engine powered the hydraulic system of the mid-upper gun turret. The loss of power meant that the turret was almost completely immobilised. Fortunately they were not approached by any night-fighters during the three-and-a-quarter hours flight back to Wyton. Selwyn succeeded in making a safe landing despite having had one of his tyres burst by shrapnel.

Encouraged by the crews' debriefing reports, Harris decided to mount an immediate repeat attack against Berlin on the following night, 23 November. To the inhabitants of the city, it became known as 'the double blow'. The accumulative effect was catastrophic, exceeding anything inflicted by Bomber Command in later raids. Extensive damage was caused in the industrial and administrative quarters, 3500 people were killed and 175,000 made homeless. The eleven major fires started on the first night were still visible through the clouds when the all-Lancaster force, 387 strong, arrived over the city on the second.

Selwyn did not take part in this raid. OL-N 'Nan' had been badly knocked about and was unfit to fly. The Squadron had no spare aircraft for him. With one exception, her crew was 'stood down' from the operation. The exception was Burton-Burgess. He was told to fly as engineer to the Squadron's new commanding officer, Wing Commander Raymond Hilton, DSO, DFC. Having no regular crew of his own, Hilton had naturally asked for the best man available. His Lancaster, OL-C   JB284, left Wyton at half past five in the evening. Four hours later, all seven crew were dead. Selwyn would need to look for a new flight engineer. The Squadron was given a new commanding officer.

One of the Elite

On 26 November they were off again, back to Berlin. This was the first occasion when Selwyn was directly involved in marking the aiming point. The load consisted of four green target indicators, a 'Cookie', and eight 500 pounders. It was planned that two aircraft fitted with H2S air-to-surface radar would identify the aiming point and mark it with yellow indicators. The 'backers up', Selwyn included, would reinforce the marking with cascades of green. The plan started to go wrong when the two primary marker aircraft ran into trouble. The situation was retrieved when Selwyn and other Pathfinder pilots realised that the yellows had been wrongly placed. The marking was still uncertain, but most of the main force bomb loads were directed into suburbs containing important factories.

18

This was the night when the Berlin Zoo was hit. Leopards, jaguars, panthers and apes broke free and were shot by hunting parties in the streets. It was also the night when, for the first and only time, the area was free of cloud. For the aircrews, most of whom had never before witnessed a major city laid out clearly below them and under attack, it was a very disturbing sight. Hundreds of searchlight beams turned night into day, exposing each aircraft and those around it. German night-fighters could be seen working their way through the stream, sending down bomber after bomber in trails of fire and exploding bomb-loads. Four miles below, the target area was a boiling cauldron of bursting bombs, blazing streets and belching gun barrels. Massed batteries of 88 mm and 128 mm flak guns were sending up a dense barrage which formed a lethal canopy along the bombers' route. The thunder of the exploding shells could be heard inside the aircraft. On the ground, sweating gun-crews served their 'eighty-eights' with a fresh shell every nine seconds and the paint peeled from the hot near-vertical barrels. No other experience could have brought home to Selwyn more strongly the enormous escalation in the bombing offensive since his first tour of operations.

His aircraft on this night was OL-Q JB114 because OL-N 'Nan' was still under repair. His crew was unchanged except for the replacement flight engineer, Flight Sergeant C Stretch. The starboard outer engine failed on the approach to the city, but Stretch helped Selwyn to continue his attack and they brought the aircraft back to Wyton without damage.

OL-N was repaired in time for the next sortie to Berlin, on 2 December, but the crew was again made up with 'spare bods'. Hewson and Sargent, and the mid-upper gunner, Victor Osterloh, were still there, but the others were strangers. An eighth and most unusual member of the team was Flight Lieutenant Frank Forster DFM, 83 Squadron's senior flight engineer. It was unprecedented to have two flight engineers in the same aircraft. His presence is explained by the fact that Sergeant W S Travers, the replacement for Stretch, was fresh out of training and making his debut appearance over Germany. Forster was there to keep an eye on him. It is possible that he was also assessing the performance of the pilot. Selwyn would soon be awarded his Pathfinder Force Badge and, with time and greater experience, might even be considered for elevation to 'primary marker' status.

This latest attack on Berlin was spoiled by inaccurate wind forecasts. Some damage was caused to industrial premises, but the bombing was scattered and mainly ineffectual. Forty bombers, 8.7% of the force, were shot down. Amongst the casualties were two newspaper reporters who had gone on the raid to gain a first-hand impression.

Within twenty-four hours of returning from their exhausting trip to Berlin, the crews were back in the air. The destination this time was the important industrial city of Leipzig. The buildings erected before the war for the World Fair, and including the largest single-span structure ever built, had been adapted for the production of Junkers bombers. It was a long haul, over seven hours, and the target was covered by the usual thick cloud, but the bombing inflicted great damage. A thousand people were killed on the ground and Bomber Command lost 150 aircrew. The World Fair complex was wrecked.

The next 'maximum effort' came on 16 December. Selwyn was lucky to be stood down this night. The bombers met very bad weather over Europe and thick fog over England when they returned. Of the 481 Lancasters despatched, twenty-five were forced to turn back, twenty-five were shot down, and twenty-eight crashed while trying to land. Four more were abandoned by their crews who could not find anywhere to land and so took to their parachutes.

One of those lost was a Lancaster from 83 Squadron. Flown by Flight Lieutenant F E McLean, JB344 had been hit over Berlin and all its communications equipment destroyed. Somehow the navigator managed to find his way back to Wyton. Unable to talk with the ground controllers and with only a few minutes' worth of petrol left in the tanks, McLean decided to let down through the fog and attempt a blind landing. At 200 feet, banking hard and his wing tip perilously close to the ground, he narrowly missed another Lancaster which was making its final straight-and-level approach over the perimeter fence. This aircraft, OL-F JB453, flown by Flight Lieutenant Joe Northrop DFC AFC, hit the 'wash' from McLean's Lancaster and was thrown off course. Bashing its way through the tops of several trees, it climbed slowly back to a safe altitude. Half an hour later, 'having simmered down somewhat', Northrop managed to get down in one piece. The other crew was not so fortunate. Their Lancaster hit a tree, struck the ground, broke up and caught fire. Three men were killed and four others injured in various degrees. Two of the survivors, McLean and Sergeant R A Lindsay, were later decorated for having tried to save their comrades from the flames. Nearly fifty years on, the night of 16/17 December is still remembered by elderly former members of Bomber Command as 'Black Thursday'.

Selwyn's next sortie came four nights later. The target was Frankfurt and he took off with a mixed load of bombs and target indicators at five o'clock in the evening. He climbed steadily in the darkness over the North Sea and had started to cross Holland when the starboard outer engine showed signs of stress. It was shut down and he turned back to Wyton. With only three engines turning, he would have reached Frankfurt long after the other Pathfinders and been unable, therefore, to mark the target. It was not a good night for Bomber Command. Forty aircraft were shot down and only limited damage inflicted on the city.

On 23 December a modest force of 370 bombers, mainly Lancasters, tried to maintain the onslaught on Berlin despite appalling weather. The bombing was scattered and ineffective, mainly because the red target indicators released by the leading Pathfinders could not be seen through the thick cloud. Little is known of Selwyn's contribution to the marking, but it is unlikely to have been accurate. While he was running in to the aiming point, his faithful OL-N 'Nan' was hit by several incendiary bombs. They had been released by another Lancaster flying at a higher altitude. No onboard fires broke out, but 'Nan' was badly damaged and once more returned to the maintenance hangar for repair.

Six days later came the order to attack Berlin again. Although allocated a different aircraft, OL-L JB461, this was one of only two occasions when Selwyn flew with an unchanged crew. Loaded with target indicators, incendiary bombs and a Cookie, they set off with 711 other bombers for the long haul across Europe. Harris had ordered a complex route and various diversionary tactics to confuse the German night-fighter controllers. The ruse was successful, and Selwyn had no trouble, but the attack itself was a failure. Residential areas on the city's eastern and southern fringes were hit, but nothing of importance.

Christmas had come and gone, and the crews were facing a New Year which offered no prospect of a slackening in the brutal pace. Dense cloud formations over Germany, day after day, prevented the high flying photographic reconnaissance Spitfires and Mosquitoes from taking any pictures of the ground. It was impossible for the British to assess the effect of the bombardment. Harris could only continue the pressure and hope that the battle was running in his favour.

Into 1944

Little is known of Selwyn's next sortie, but it seems to have been another dramatic experience. On 2 January he took OL-L JB461 once again to Berlin, lifting off from Wyton shortly after midnight. Approaching the city, he found uninterrupted cloud reaching up to 19,000 feet. Pathfinders ahead of him were dropping red and green parachute flares in an attempt to mark the aiming point, but these were quickly swallowed by the grey blanket below. Berlin was not an easy target to identify by airborne radar alone, so the attack was bound to be a hit-or-miss affair. Selwyn levelled up for his bombing run and handed over nominal control of the aircraft to Flight Sergeant D Wildon, a bomb aimer who was flying with him for the first time. It was Wildon's job to direct his captain to the dropping point: 'OK, keep her steady, left a bit, left, left steady, hold it, hold it, right a bit, right, OK, steady, steady'. At this critical moment the Lancaster was bracketed by an accurate salvo of 88 mm flak. The cloud did not interfere with the work of the German ground radar operators. They could easily follow the head of the bomber stream as it came in over the city. Selwyn's OL-L made a good clear 'blip' on their screens. Like all Pathfinders, he could not hide himself in the anonymity of the following main force.

Nothing is known of the damage inflicted, but Selwyn was forced to break off the bombing run and head for a quieter patch of sky. Wildon jettisoned his load over open country and OL-L headed back westwards. Selwyn touched down at Wyton a full hour later than the other aircraft of 83 Squadron. It must have been a close brush with what was always sardonically called 'the chop' — that final flight from which there was no return.

The battered OL-N 'Nan' was patched up in time for the Squadron's next operation, a raid on the Baltic port of Stettin. Being a coastal city, it showed up much more clearly on the H2S radar screen than the amorphous mass of Berlin. Even better, there were some gaps in the cloud cover when Selwyn and the other markers arrived, precisely as planned, at twenty minutes to four in the morning. As the shower of flares and markers went down, he and his bomb aimer, Flight Sergeant Highet, could see details of buildings and the surrounding snow-covered countryside. It was an unusual and satisfying experience. Several major fires were started in Stettin's commercial centre and eight ships were sunk in the harbour. The German night-fighters had expected yet another raid on Berlin and were waiting there for a bomber force which never appeared. Most of the twelve Lancasters and two Halifaxes lost over Stettin were shot down by flak. OL-N came home unscathed.

During all this time, Selwyn was taking whatever opportunities he could to visit Dorothy and his parents at Brockmoor. They were precious moments, a day here and a couple of days there, which gave him the chance to relax in the peaceful atmosphere of the Vicarage and the village. He and his new wife had been able to spend so little time together since they had first met, three years earlier, that there was still much which they did not know about each other. It was, in many ways, a typical bitter-sweet wartime marriage.

At Wyton, when the Squadron was not operating, or when snow and fog prevented test flying, all crew members were occupied with lectures, with catching up on their sleep, and with the routine of the Daily Inspections on their aircraft. The 'DI' was a complete check on every electrical and mechanical system, ensuring that it had not developed any faults since the previous day. Responsibility for this task lay with the ground crews, who did the practical work, but aircrew were required to visit their aircraft daily and to take advice from the ground crew regarding any potential problems.

Except for major overhauls, all repair and maintenance work was performed in the open air. Wyton had approximately fifty aircraft dispersed around its perimeter. Half of these were the Lancasters of 83 Squadron, the other half being Mosquito light bombers of 139 (Jamaica) Squadron. It was impossible to keep such a large number of aircraft under cover. The ground crews, therefore, were obliged to carry out their duties, including such major tasks as engine changes, while fully exposed to wind, rain and snow. If time allowed, they took shelter for 'a brew and a drag' in the make-shift shacks which they built for themselves alongside 'their' Lancaster or 'their' Mosquito.

The life of the ground crews was highly demanding and not always officially recognised. The least mistake on the part of one mechanic could lead directly to the deaths of seven aircrew, a fact which every rigger and fitter had always in his mind. And no matter how efficient they were, they knew that sooner or later 'their' aircraft, and the crew with whom they were joking a few hours earlier, would fail to return. Aircraft and aircrew came and went, but the ground crews were the permanent heart and soul of the Squadron.

At Bomber Command headquarters, at High Wycombe, a sense of anxiety was developing. Losses were increasing all the time, but there was still no certainty that the assault on Berlin was having the planned effect. The city's flak defences were ever more efficient, and the Luftwaffe was consistently assembling large numbers of night-fighters well in advance of the bomber stream's arrival.

New Lancasters were rolling off the production lines in sufficient numbers to replace the losses and to equip new squadrons, but too many of the best and most experienced crews had been killed. Many of those who remained were needed as instructors to train the hundreds of youngsters in the operational training units. The average age of aircrew had fallen from twenty-four to twenty-one. Many were even younger. It was not uncommon for a heavy bomber pilot to have not yet learned to drive a motor car.

Harris decided to give his squadrons a chance to catch their breath. His attention shifted to other, theoretically less well defended, targets. Stettin had been hammered, now it was the turn of Brunswick. In the late afternoon of 15 January, 83 Squadron took off from Wyton for a raid which became a severe defeat for the British.

German radar stations detected the bomber stream as it crossed the English coast. The alert was flashed across Northern Europe. Night-fighter bases and flak batteries from Belgium to Denmark prepared themselves for yet another major aerial battle. Which way would the bombers go? While the Luftwaffe controllers assessed the reports coming in from the radar network, their fighters were already inserting themselves into the stream.

Brunswick was correctly identified as the target. Thirty-eight of the attacking 673 bombers were shot down. Eleven of these were Pathfinders. Selwyn was lucky. He dropped his indicators and Cookie on time, and reported that the attack had been successful. Post-war analysis showed that most of the bombs had instead fallen in open country to the south of the city. Brunswick suffered no more than ten houses blown up and fourteen civilians killed. The RAF lost 266 of its best aviators. Technical advances in the German defence system, and the bravery of the night-fighter crews, were proving almost insuperable. Harris was not yet ready to give up, but the events of the next few weeks were to prove even more disastrous for his campaign.

Berlin was back on the agenda on 20 January. Selwyn was flying OL-S JA967, a new Mark III with improved radar. Yet another Flight Engineer, Sgt R Richardson, was in charge of the 'cocks and tits', as the engineering controls were cheerfully known, but the others were men with whom he always flew or who had joined him on previous sorties: Eric Sargent, Les Davis, H C Highet, Victor Osterloh, and Bill Hewson. Despite heavy icing and solid cloud reaching up from almost ground level to 14,000 feet, the flight went well. OL-S avoided any involvement with flak or fighters and arrived promptly over Berlin just after eleven o'clock. Selwyn reported later that he had seen his red target indicators and green flares going down as ordered. In the event, the main force bombing went badly astray. German sources make no reference to any significant damage on this night.

Weather reports suggested some improvement over Germany for the following night. Harris decided to mount another maximum effort, the target this time being the important industrial city of Magdeburg. It was on the route to Berlin, so perhaps the Germans could be deceived into sending all of their night fighters to the capital instead of defending the true target. The ruse failed. German electronic experts had some time earlier learned to detect a distant bomber stream by homing onto the emissions of each bomber's radar equipment. The British, unaware of the advances made by German scientists, were effectively signalling their intentions almost as soon as they took off. On this night, German fighters were in the stream and hacking down bombers even before they completed the North Sea crossing. The slaughter continued for the next five hours. Of 648 Lancasters and Halifaxes despatched, fifty-seven were lost. The overall loss rate for the force was 8.8%, while for the Halifaxes, flying at lower altitudes, it was a calamitous 15.6%.

Selwyn had been allocated another Lancaster, OL-C JB352. Apart from the flight engineer, the crew had all flown with him before. It would be a shorter trip than usual, the omens for a successful raid were good. Bad weather, however, again played havoc with the plan.

Winds much stronger than those forecast brought many of the main force bombers to Magdeburg before the Pathfinders had had time to identify the aiming point and to mark it. Incendiaries started some early fires, generating smoke which hid the winking red and green lights of the target indicators. With night-fighters in amongst them, with other bombers burning and exploding all around them, few of the RAF crews were willing to stay long in the area. The bombing was widely scattered and little damage was caused. A captured British airman, held in a city centre hospital, later reported having heard 'some bangs, far away'. For this, nearly 400 Commonwealth airmen were lost.

Four Englishmen

And so we come to the events of 27 January 1944. Before describing Selwyn Alcock's last flight, it is appropriate to look at the careers of the men who flew with him. They were, in most ways, a typical cross-section of the aircrews who comprised the backbone of the Pathfinder Force at that stage of the war. In reading these pages, it is important to keep in mind the fact that every man was a volunteer. Even though the severe losses in Bomber Command were a matter of public knowledge, there had been no slackening in the flow of young men coming forward and asking to be trained as aviators. A later generation must feel humble in the face of such selfless

W/Cdr John Searby (seated, centre) poses with some of his crews at RAF Wyton shortly before leaving 83 Sqn in October 1943. Standing, extreme left, is Bill Hewson. Fourth from the left, in the same row, is Selwyn Alcock. The Lancaster in the background, OL-Q JB114, was lost with all her crew in a mid-air collision over Zehrensdorf, near Berlin, on the night of 1 January 1944.

enthusiasm to accept the near certainty of capture, injury or violent death.

The target this night would be, once more, 'the big city'. The aircraft assigned was another new Lancaster, OL-V 'Victor', JB724. The crew which reported for briefing at Wyton that afternoon was Flight Lieutenant Selwyn Alcock (pilot), Sergeant Stanley Bullamore (flight engineer), Flight Lieutenant Eric Sargent DFC (navigator), Flight Lieutenant Leslie Davis (wireless operator), Flying Officer Robert Adamson RCAF (bomb aimer), Warrant Officer Victor Osterloh (mid-upper gunner), and Flying Officer Bill Hewson RAAF (rear gunner).

In paying tribute to these men, it would be fitting to write something about their origins and pre-war lives. This is not the easy task which it might seem. The historian is faced with the obstacles imposed by the United Kingdom's inscrutable Official Secrets Act and the Public Record Act. The authorities will not reveal any information of any kind regarding those who fought in the service of their homeland. The only exception to this rule is the case when an immediate family descendant requests such information. Even then, the details are heavily edited.

Successive British governments have failed to recognise the irony of this stringently imposed secrecy. Nearly 55,000 young men were killed while flying with Bomber Command. Most of them, if not all, believed that they were fighting to preserve an open and democratic way of life. Australian, New Zealand and Canadian airmen were justified in that belief. Their British comrades were not.

Dominion governments take the view that a former serviceman's record should be within the public domain provided that it could not in any way cause distress or embarrassment to him or his family. The Mother of Parliaments takes a contrary view. As a consequence, the dedication and sacrifice of tens of thousands of British-born servicemen will remain unrecognised until at least the middle of the 21st Century. Four of Selwyn's crew come within this category, hence they will endure as little more than names on headstones.

Despite the barriers erected by officialdom, some details of Les Davis's earlier flying career have been traced. It is known that his first tour of operations was served with 106 Squadron, at RAF Syerston, where he flew with Wing Commander John Searby DFC. He moved to 83 Squadron when Searby was appointed to command it in May 1943. He continued to fly with him throughout that summer and early autumn, transferring to Selwyn Alcock's crew only when Searby was promoted away as a Group Captain in October.

Davis must have been an outstanding wireless operator. John Searby, who survived the war as an Air Commodore, was an exceptional pilot, leader and disciplinarian. He is still remembered by those who knew him with an admiration verging upon awe. After retirement, he wrote three books based largely upon his experiences with 106 and 83 Squadron. Selwyn was lucky indeed to inherit one of the men who had met Searby's standards and earned his confidence.

Les Davis flew five 83 Squadron sorties with Searby in May, June and July of 1943. The fifth of these was the Hamburg raid of 24 July. The weather was poor at Wyton when the bombers returned. Searby's report stated: 'I called up permission to land and was given a (holding) height of 1000 feet as the runway was in use. From this height, on the crosswind leg, I could barely make out the flarepath. Suddenly, coming towards me out of the gloom, a black shape appeared immediately ahead. I thrust the control column forward and there was a horrible crunch as the black shape sliced off the mid-upper turret. Fortunately, the gunner had made a timely exit a few seconds before. The controls were badly damaged. I was given a priority landing. It was later reported that the other Lancaster involved in the mid-air collision was that of Squadron Leader S Hall of 156 Squadron. He also landed safely, with the starboard outer engine on fire and dangling from the wing'.

Having survived this encounter by the narrowest margin, Les Davis had an even more testing experience on 17 August. This was the night of the famous attack on the experimental rocket testing station at Peenemunde. It was the first time that the Pathfinder Force provided a Master Bomber to direct and control the placement of markers and the bombing effort of the main force. The officer selected for the task was John Searby. His radio man, Les Davis, had the vital task of keeping open the communication channels to the hundreds of other aircraft as they streamed in over the Baltic. Searby made seven passes over the target, talking calmly all the time and telling other crews where to drop their loads. German night fighters arrived in large numbers as the raid progressed. Dozens of combats were fought in the brilliant light generated by the burning target. For fifty minutes, Searby cruised through this maelstrom, even shaking off an attack on his own Lancaster. Surprisingly, Davis was not decorated for his work this night.

After John Searby's departure from the Squadron, Les moved to the crew of another veteran pilot, Flight Lieutenant F J Garvey DFC. They flew ten sorties together during the autumn months, with raids on Hannover, Stuttgart, Kassel, Mannheim and Berlin. These sorties were all flown in OL-Q   JB114. The aircraft was lost on the Berlin raid of New Year's Day, but by then Les had been moved to Selwyn Alcock's crew. They were destined to fly only three operations together, but Selwyn must have been delighted to have the services of such a very experienced wireless operator.

Attempts to make contact with the families of the other Englishmen who flew with him that night have met with no success. Nearly two generations have come and gone since the war of 1939-1945. Parents have died, brothers and sisters have become elderly and moved away to other addresses. Being so young, very few of the aircrew left behind them children who otherwise would have perpetuated their names. Picking up the trail at this distance in time is a quest too frequently doomed to frustration.

Victor Osterloh, the mid-upper gunner, seems to have been an orphan. His Germanic surname has been traced to a cabinet maker who emigrated from Bremen under peculiar circumstances in the 1860s and settled in London. A number of the descendants can be found in London, Hampshire and Devon, but Victor himself was raised in Chiswick by a guardian who must have died many years ago. His rank of Warrant Officer indicates that he had almost certainly served a first tour with another unit before joining 83 Squadron in September 1943, but no details of his earlier service have been traced.

The new man in the crew, Stanley Bullamore, the flight engineer, was from Hull, Yorkshire. His mother, a widow, lived at 39 Marlow Street, a working class district of that city. A recent local radio appeal has failed to generate a response from any surviving relatives.

Stanley had arrived at RAF Wyton on the morning of 27 January straight from an operational training unit. Presumably he had qualified at the head of his course and, for this reason, been hand-picked for the Pathfinders. This was his first front-line posting. He reported himself at the Guardroom but, before he had time to find a billet and unpack his bags, was told that he was needed for a test flight with Flight Lieutenant Alcock. Twelve hours later he was dead.

Eric Sargent, the navigator, was a second-tour man and had already flown fifteen sorties with Selwyn. His father was a retired army officer and the family lived in the comfortable London suburb of Blackheath. Twelve months earlier he had been awarded the Distinguished Flying Cross while serving with 37 Squadron in the Middle East. This unit had been equipped with Wellington bombers shortly before the outbreak of war and had suffered catastrophic losses while trying to operate along the German coast in daylight. It moved to Egypt in November 1940, and Eric Sargent's award was recognition of his thirty-nine sorties to Crete and over the Western Desert.

A Canadian

The Canadian bomb aimer, Bob Adamson, was born and raised in the prairie village of Innisfree, Alberta. Much like the Belgian village where he is now commemorated, it had a population of little more than 200 souls, mainly farmers and artisans. He was the first child of Morris Adamson, the local doctor, and his wife, Minnie. Five children followed him, a girl and two sets of twin boys. Douglas, one of the older twins and four years junior, also joined the Royal Canadian Air Force. He was killed on 14 March 1944 while on a routine training flight in England. The aircraft in which he was flying came down a mile west of Abingdon airfield. His grave is to be found in the Commonwealth War Graves Commission cemetery at Botley, North Hinksey, near Oxford. He survived his elder brother by just twelve weeks.

Bob graduated from the local two-room school house with a university entrance acceptance. His ambition was to follow in his father's footsteps and

The five Adamson boys, with a friend, celebrate a Royal visit to Alberta in 1939. Douglas, who will die in 1944, stands at the right of the picture. Bob, waving the Union flag, will be lost in that same year.

Bob Adamson, in 1941, age 20, when he was a newly promoted Sergeant Observer.

become a medical practitioner once the war was over. His parents had encouraged him to develop both physically and mentally under the big skies of Western Canada. He became a fine marksman and athlete, excelling at hockey. His father had served with the Canadian Expeditionary Force in Russia in 1919, so it is not surprising that Bob decided to volunteer for war service as soon as he was able. In July 1942 he enlisted at Edmonton and followed the well-trodden path through the RCAF initial training schools at Mossbank, Regina, Virden and Souris. In August 1941, just past his twentieth birthday, he embarked for the United Kingdom.

Nothing is known of his travels during the next two years because he was serving with the Royal Air Force, not the Royal Canadian Air Force. His record is therefore still regarded, by the British Ministry of Defence, as a national secret. He will have spent some time in the United Kingdom with various training units, building his bomb aiming skills on elderly Whitleys or Wellingtons, before joining a front-line operational squadron (it is not known which one). He will have completed a tour of thirty or more sorties, over a period of five or six months, and then been 'rested' for a while as an instructor. All that is known for certain is that he joined 83 Squadron on 7 January 1944 from the Pathfinder Force Navigation Training Unit. Assigned to Selwyn Alcock's crew, he replaced Flight Sergeant Highet (who was presumably 'tour expired'). Bob Adamson flew only two trips with Selwyn, the second being the one from which they did not return.

And an Australian

It is the Australian government to which we are most indebted for some understanding of the individuals who flew with Bomber Command. The following account of Bill Hewson's life and times is based upon official records, his family's memories, and his own Flying Log Book. It serves to demonstrate what is still concealed in the British archives.

William Henry Hewson was born in Sydney on 15 April 1912 and was therefore nearly thirty-two years of age at the time of the Berlin raids. This made him considerably older than the youngsters with whom he flew. By trade he was an electrical fitter, but the Depression of the 1930s caused as much hardship to him as it did for millions of others around the world. Jobs were scarce and life was hard. Even so, in 1936 he married Betty Abbotsmith and they settled in Bexley North, Victoria. Soon they had two sons, Alan and John.

Bill is described by his widow as a cheerful extrovert man, strongly built and physically very fit. He followed the Australian tradition of spending much time out-of-doors, camping, hunting and fishing. He was a member of the 34th Battalion Volunteer Militia, in which he held the rank of Sergeant, and was a leading member of the Sutherland Rifle Club. A first-class shot, he won many shooting competitions and top awards. When the crisis came in 1939, he was happily married, had two young sons, a regular job on the maintenance staff of Toohey's Brewery, and was a well-established member of his local community. Putting all that to one side, he volunteered for service overseas. The decision was entirely his own. Conscription, and then only on a limited basis, was not introduced in Australia until 1943.

He resigned his job at the brewery and was enlisted into the Royal Australian Air Force on 24 May 1941. After six months of basic training, he was selected for further training as an air gunner. As a qualified electrician he might have been channelled into one of the ground crew trades, or trained as a wireless operator, but presumably his proven weaponry skills swung the balance. Together with other embryo aircrew, he embarked at Sydney for San Francisco. Their destination was Canada where the Empire Air Training Scheme was expanding rapidly to produce thousands of new aircrew for the Royal Air Force.

The SS *Monterey*, a luxury liner, sailed serenely across the Pacific and reached Honolulu, Hawaii, on 1 December 1941. She remained in the port for five days, then sailed for America. Forty-eight hours later the Japanese launched their devastating air attack which brought the United States into the war. For Bill Hewson and his companions, a high adventure had suddenly become a deadly serious commitment.

The spring and summer of 1942 were spent at the Royal Canadian Air Force gunnery schools at Fingal, Ontario, and at Stormy Downs. He received his 'AG' brevet in August, having trained on obsolescent Battles, Whitleys and Defiants and having passed with exceptionally high marks. He was recommended to be an instructor, once he had completed a tour of operations. He was by now a Pilot Officer (AG), having received his Commission in May.

Arriving in England in September, he went to RAF Harwell for intensive training on the Wellington bomber. This period was followed by two months at RAF Riccall, training on the larger Halifax. His Flying Log shows a succession of training flights all over the British Isles with a pilot by the name of Sergeant Dickinson. They were working up to the point at which they would be passed fit for operational duties.

Dickinson's crew, instead of joining one of the Bomber Command units in England, was ordered to the Middle East. A previously disbanded Wellington unit, 148 Squadron, was being reformed at Gambut, halfway between Tobruk and Bardia on the Egyptian-Libyan border. It was designated a 'Special Operations' squadron, equipped with Halifaxes and Liberators. These long-range four-engined types were ideal for delivering agents and supplies to the Partisan bands fighting the Germans and Italians in the Balkans.

Dickinson and his crew left Portreath, Cornwall, on 21 February 1943 for their long and lonely haul down to the Mediterranean. It involved nearly nine hours' flying across the Bay of Biscay to Gibraltar and then, fitted with extra fuel tanks, nearly thirteen hours to touch-down at a landing strip in the Western Desert. The aircraft was a twin-engined Wellington, not an ideal means of passing through skies where roving Junkers 88s might be met at any time.

Dickinson and Hewson were already qualified to operate the Halifax. After a brief period of acclimatisation, they were sent on a leaflet-dropping sortie to Greece. If the officer commanding 148 Squadron thought that he was giving the new crew an easy introduction to their future duties, events proved him wrong. The Halifax was greeted by heavy flak and was intercepted by a night-fighter.

For the first and only time in his operational career, Bill Hewson fired his guns at an enemy aircraft. His Log records the discharge of forty rounds, a very brief burst indeed. Presumably he had only a fleeting sight of the attacker. Certainly the sortie must have been difficult. When the Halifax touched down at Gambut, it had been airborne for ten hours and fifteen minutes, a long time for a round trip to Greece.

In the space of eighteen weeks, Bill and his comrades completed thirty-nine solitary flights by night across the Mediterranean. They were allocated Halifax BB381, later replaced by BB387. The task was to deliver weapons, secret agents and military advisers by parachute into Greece, Yugoslavia and Albania. The Squadron was mounting up to ninety such sorties every month. It was, by any standard, dangerous work. It involved crossing a wide expanse of sea where there was no prospect of rescue if they were forced down. It involved flying at low altitude over, and between, badly-mapped mountains. And it involved finding small clusters of beacons laid out by the Partisans, as dropping zones, with no supporting ground navigational aids.

The Halifax was not designed to operate from dusty desert airstrips. Keeping the aircraft serviceable under these conditions posed many problems. The crews lived under canvas, with monotonous food and rationed water supplies. By August, Dickinson's crew was more than ready for a rest. Bill Hewson returned to England and, after a short leave, was posted to RAF Honeybourne pending a return to operations. He now had a total of 487 flying hours in his Log, 362 of which were night flying. It is remarkable that such an experienced gunner was not employed, at least for a few months, as an instructor. It may be that he was keen to join the big league and managed to 'wangle' a swift posting to 83 Squadron.

When Bill reached Wyton on 10 September 1943, he had already teamed up with Selwyn Alcock. They did not immediately fly together. It will be remembered that Selwyn began his second tour by flying as a 'second dickey'. Bill, therefore, was assigned temporarily to other pilots. In the space of ten days he flew on four raids. It was not the gentle introduction to Northern Europe for which he might have been hoping.

On 16 September he went as rear gunner to Squadron Leader C A J Smith DFC in OL-E JA701 to bomb the Mont Cenis railway tunnel in the French Alps. Four nights later he again crewed with Smith for a raid on Hannover. Both sorties were trouble-free.

Bill Hewson (standing) with an unknown friend, a photograph probably taken shortly after his arrival in England from the Middle East in August 1943.

The harsh realities of night operations over Germany came on 23 September. With Pilot Officer D N Britton as pilot, he went in OL-F ED602 to Darmstadt. The bomb aimer had difficulty in identifying the aiming point, so Britton made three successive runs across the target area to give him a good 'fix'. Almost inevitably, the aircraft was hit by flak. The extent of the damage is not known, but Britton needed an hour more than the other pilots to get back to Wyton.

Bill's experiences on 26 September were even more alarming. He was rear gunner in OL-N EE201, flown by Pilot Officer J Finding. Their target for the night was Hannover. Winds were much stronger than those forecast. The bomber stream became scattered and therefore easy meat for night-fighters and flak batteries alike. Approaching the target, near Steinhuder Meer, OL-N was caught by an accurate salvo of 88 mm shells. The explosions blew away the forward escape hatch. An instant rush of air, caused by the aircraft's 160 miles per hour slipstream, sucked all of the navigator's maps and his flight log out into the night sky. The inter-communication system, by which the crew talked to each other, failed completely. To maintain contact, the five men in the cabin area removed their helmets and face masks so that they could shout into each other's ears. Apart from the probability of frostbite, they were running the risk of oxygen starvation.

Finding told the others that he was aborting the attack on Hannover. Instead, he reduced height and turned towards the known location of a Luftwaffe airfield, at Havern. The bomb load was released on a 'dead reckoning' basis. There is no record of where eventually it fell.

Even before the bomb doors could be closed, the Lancaster was hit yet again by a salvo of radar-predicted flak. As a single isolated aircraft, the Lancaster made a juicy clear 'blip' on the German ground radar screens. More holes were torn in the airframe and the radar navigation system was smashed. Good co-operation between the crew was maintained during all this excitement and the navigator, Sergeant H E Barrow, gave his pilot a course to steer for home. This was based upon nothing more than reference to the DR compass and his memory of their earlier position.

Flying blindly back towards England, the big bomber strayed over the heavily defended city of Osnabrück and was twice 'coned' by groups of searchlights. The pilot each time dived and twisted and turned to escape the cage of blinding light. Huddled in his rear turret, Bill Hewson was hurled from side to side and bounced violently up and down as Finding threw the Lancaster around the sky. The effect of each manoeuvre was multiplied by his position at the aircraft's rear extremity. The long fuselage acted as a whip, with Bill at its tip. He had no way of knowing what was happening in the cabin, or whether perhaps the other members of the crew were already taking to their parachutes.

Losing several thousand feet of altitude in the process, Finding broke through the searchlight belt and resumed his guesswork course for England. By 1943 the RAF had an efficient ground control system to guide lost or damaged aircraft back to their bases or to an emergency landing field. The wireless operator in OL-N,

Flight Sergeant W Bainbridge, began sending out distress calls as they crossed over the North Sea and approached the English coast. The roar of the slipstream rushing through the length of the Lancaster was such that he could hear nothing in his headphones. Only by watching the flickering needles and dials as they reacted to signals from ground stations could he and the navigator calculate their probable position. By hand signs and scribbled notes, they guided their pilot to Catfoss, a forward emergency airfield on the East Yorkshire coast.

Several searchlights were switched on by ground staff to show him the way, but Finding was faced with thick cloud extending down to 300 feet from the ground. This was only three times more than the Lancaster's wingspan. It provided no margin for error or low level changes in course. Worse, having had no reports of local barometric pressures since leaving Wyton, he could not even trust his own altimeter. After several aborted attempts, he nursed OL-N down to a safe landing. It was not only a very skilled arrival, it was an extremely lucky one. Bill Hewson and some of the others found that they had incurred mild frostbite to their hands and faces, but they were otherwise unharmed.

Bill did not fly again until 13 October when he made a short training flight with Selwyn Alcock in Lancaster JB309. It was allocated the call-sign OL-N 'Nan' previously carried by EE201. The OL-N in which Bill had had such an adventurous flight on 26 September was so badly damaged that it was withdrawn from service for major repairs and overhaul. The new 'Nan' would later prove to be even more of a magnet for German flak than its predecessor.

Bill Hewson's subsequent flying career was exactly the same as Selwyn's. From now on they would live together and fly together. Four months later they would die together.

Back to Berlin

Now we must return to the events of 27 January 1944. Air Marshal Harris had chaired his usual early morning staff meeting to hear the reports and opinions of his intelligence and meteorological experts. He had talked by 'scrambler' telephone with the officers commanding each of the Bomber Groups. Seventy-six aircraft had been despatched during the night to attack V-1 weapon launching sites in the Pas de Calais and near Cherbourg. All had returned safely. Eight Mosquitoes had kept the German defences on their toes by dropping Cookies on the border city of Aachen. Eighteen Wellingtons with freshman crews had been sent by operational training units to drop leaflets over France. For the rest, Bomber Command had enjoyed a quiet night, the fourth in a row.

Conditions of moon and weather looked promising for yet another major assault on the German capital. Much of the battle damage inflicted on Harris's aircraft during the Magdeburg raid had been made good, or would be during the next few hours. New aircraft had been flown in from the maintenance units to replace those recently shot down. New crews had arrived from the operational training units and heavy conversion units. An enormous production line, supplying machines, men and munitions to the bomber squadrons, and involving tens of thousands of civilian workers and RAF ground staff, had repaired and resharpened the mighty weapon which was Bomber Command.

Station commanders reported the numbers of aircraft they expected to have 'on top line' by the afternoon. Harris made his decision. The target for tonight would be, once again, 'the big city'. By midday, the teleprinters were chattering out the coded details of the most complex plan yet devised by his staff.

The announcement that they would be flying that night sent the crews out to the dispersals soon after breakfast. It was standard practice to 'air test' each aircraft before despatching it on a raid. This involved no more than a short flight of twenty to thirty minutes over the local countryside to check systems and to identify any 'gremlins' which might be lurking in the machinery. Unfortunately, the German monitoring stations along the coast of Europe were capable of detecting the sharply increased levels of radio traffic which accompanied all these testing flights. The traffic did not reveal the target, but it did alert the Germans to the fact that a big raid was likely within the coming hours.

Having satisfied themselves that OL-V 'Victor' was fully serviceable, Selwyn's crew joined all the others scheduled for the attack at a one o'clock briefing. They listened as the Squadron Commander described their role and the planned route. The 'met man' gave his sceptical audience an estimation of the night's probable weather pattern, and the Station Commander voiced his usual words of encouragement. For most of those present, it was a familiar routine. For young Stan Bullamore, however, it was a novel and worrisome business. To take part in an operation within hours of arrival on a strange squadron, especially with an unfamiliar crew and against a tough target like Berlin, was certainly not a normal procedure. Stan was nineteen years of age. The six men whose bench he shared at the briefing were his senior by only a handful of years. In practical experience, they were older by a lifetime. When Selwyn lifted OL-V 'Victor' off the tarmac at eight minutes before six o'clock, it is probable that neither he nor the other members of the crew even knew the youngster's name.

Harris's plan contained four elements. First, twenty-one Halifaxes, each equipped with H2S radar, would bomb the fortress island of Heligoland. Their powerful electronic emissions might deceive the German controllers into believing that a much larger force was heading for Kiel or some other North German target. Secondly, eighty elderly Stirlings and Wellingtons would divert attention by flying low along the Dutch coast and dropping sea mines around the Friesian Islands. Thirdly, small groups of fast moving Mosquitoes would drop flares and radar-jamming 'window' along routes leading to cities well off the Berlin track. The fourth element, the main attacking force, would follow in behind these diversions, cross over Northern Holland, move eastwards towards Kassel, but then make a final dog-leg turn for Berlin. The city was expected to be cloud-covered, as usual, so much of the briefing was devoted to the night's Pathfinder marking techniques.

After the main briefing, Selwyn's crew split up for specialist briefings of their own. Stan Bullamore, as a fledgling member of 'the plumbers union', was briefed by the Squadron engineer leader. Victor Osterloh and Bill Hewson joined the Squadron's other gunners to hear the latest 'gen' from the gunnery leader. There were similar detailed meetings for each of the other crew members, Eric Sargent with the navigators, Bob Adamson with the bombing leader, and Les Davis with the signals leader. Their discussions were in some ways the most complex. On the ground, the Germans were constructing ever more sophisticated decoy pyrotechnic displays and dummy targets to distract the navigators and bomb aimers. In the air, both sides were attempting to disrupt each other's radio traffic with jamming devices and fake instructions. The work of the Pathfinder wireless operators had become crucial to the success of an operation, even more so to the survival of their own individual aircraft.

By half past four, the crew of OL-V 'Victor' had eaten their meal of eggs and bacon (a privilege in food-rationed Britain reserved only for flying personnel), had changed into flying gear, drawn their parachutes, and were climbing out of the lorry which delivered them to their dispersal point. They walked around the Lancaster, made their usual external checks, and Selwyn signed the Form 700 offered to him by the Flight Sergeant in charge of the ground crew. 'Victor' was bombed up, fuelled and fit to fly. Now they must simply wait, each man trying to conceal his private anxieties, until the time came to start the engines.

Norman Mackie

Selwyn was in buoyant mood. Two hours earlier, as he had been leaving the Mess to collect his flying kit and parachute, he had seen someone whom he had long believed to be dead. He was Norman Mackie. The two men had joined the RAF at almost the same time and their early service careers had followed almost identical tracks. As POA (Potential Officer Aircrew) they had studied and been Commissioned together at the RAF College, Cranwell, had flown Oxfords, Ansons and Hampdens while training at RAF Cottesmore, and had both been posted to 83 Squadron at Scampton.

Much of their off-duty time was spent in each other's company. Teaming up with other 83 and 49 Squadron friends, they lost no opportunity to seek out any local pub which offered a piano and a good supply of beer. Their favourite watering holes were The Saracen's Head and The Albion in the cathedral city of Lincoln. As Norman recalls: 'Most of the 5 Group boys used to gather in these places and then go on to the Assembly Rooms if there was a dance. It was said, only half jokingly, that if you wanted to know the target for tonight, all you needed to do was ask Mary in the Snake Pit bar!'.

Norman had completed his first tour on Hampdens and Manchesters, been awarded the DFC in 1942, and then converted to Lancasters. On 12 March 1943, his luck ran out. Returning from a raid on Stuttgart, his aircraft was attacked by a night-fighter and set on fire. He managed to maintain control long enough for the surviving members of the crew to bail out. Two were killed, two taken prisoner, and two evaded capture. They later reached Spain via the Resistance system. Norman, the last to jump, got out at low level and landed near the village of Heiltz-le-Hut, south of Verdun. He was captured after twenty-four hours on the run.

His German guards removed his boots and locked him in a temporary cell. Climbing through the window, he made off in his stockinged feet and walked for several miles before friendly French civilians gave him a pair of shoes and a boiler suit to cover his RAF battle-dress. More cross-country walking led to an encounter with a Gendarme who introduced him into the Resistance network. Three weeks later he crossed the border into Switzerland.

Norman worked for six months in the office of the British Air Attaché in Berne. He was then given permission to cross back into France and try his luck at reaching Gibraltar. There followed a series of adventures which not only reflect the courage and determination of the man but which would also fill a book. With a South African pilot as companion, he got through the Pyrenees, survived a rough spell in a Spanish jail, and finally arrived back in England on 16 January 1944. After de-briefing and attending to family matters, he went to Wyton on the afternoon of 27 January to find any familiar faces which might still be there. The first one he saw was Selwyn's. 'Good Lord, what are you doing here? I thought you'd got the chop! Look, can't stop now, I'm flying tonight. Tell me all about it in the morning. Then we can celebrate'. With that, Selwyn was gone. The two friends would not meet again.

Nothing Heard from this Aircraft

Take off and the long steady climb over the North Sea followed the usual pattern. As the bomber stream crossed the Dutch coast it picked up a tail wind which pushed it quickly eastwards. The earlier deceptions had caused the Luftwaffe to send many of its fighters, based in Denmark, Germany and Holland, north to the Heligoland Bight. They shot down one Stirling, but failed to catch up with the fast moving Lancasters. These arrived over Berlin with few losses, and were greeted by a flak barrage less fierce than on previous occasions. The ground defences had been caught by surprise.

The city was covered by solid cloud, with big cumulo nimbus heads reaching up to 14,000 feet. Above that, visibility was excellent. As the first of the 440 bombers began to thunder over the outer suburbs, their crews could see that they had the sky

RAF Oakington, 1944. Norman Mackie with his navigator, F/O Angus McDonald DFC DFM RAAF, in front of their Mosquito and a 400 pounder Cookie. Half a century later, he recalled those days when he thanked the people of Sautour for their remembrance of his fallen comrades and especially of his great friend, Selwyn Alcock.

to themselves. Few German fighters appeared during the opening phase of the raid. In OL-V 'Victor', Bob Adamson fixed his bomb sight on the flares dropped by the 'primary markers' and released a salvo of red indicators and bombs. Selwyn held the big bomber steady for thirty seconds to allow the flash camera to do its job of recording the release point. The chances of obtaining a useful target picture were negligible with so much cloud in the area, but there would be disapproving noises at Wyton if he did not make the attempt.

As soon as the flash exploded, Selwyn hauled 'Victor' away to starboard and began the return leg. The route led southwards over the lightly-defended forests and mountains of Central Germany and then directly eastwards over the Rhine towards the southern extremity of Belgium and Northern France. The bomber stream would cross the Channel between Le Touquet and Eastbourne before flying up the length of England to disperse amongst its dozens of home bases. Selwyn must have felt confident. The attack had gone well, 'Victor' had sustained no damage, and the tactic of drawing night-fighters away to the north had been largely successful.

'Victor' throbbed steadily homewards at 20,000 feet and a constant 160 miles per hour. There was always the temptation to 'stick the nose down and go like a bat out of Hell', but that meant burning off fuel which might be needed later if for any reason the landing at Wyton was delayed. It also meant leaving the bomber stream. Aircraft which strayed from the pack were often the ones which 'got the chop'. It was safer to be patient and wait for the hours to tick by.

Like every experienced pilot, Selwyn knew that this stage of a sortie was in some ways the most dangerous. It was too easy to relax, to feel thankful that the attack was behind them, and to start thinking of tomorrow. The Thermos and 'the bottle' were passed around, but he checked regularly on the inter-com to make certain that each member of the crew was alert. Apart from tiredness, a lonely gunner might become drowsy, or even die, if a fault developed in his oxygen supply.

Young Bullamore was keeping a watchful eye, just as he had been so recently trained to do, on the petrol gauges, oil pressures, engine temperatures and revolutions.

Eric Sargent, screened behind the curtain of his cubby-hole, was calculating the ever changing position and drift of the aircraft, emerging only occasionally to take a star sight from the astrodome.

Les Davis, in his own small compartment, maintained constant listening watch on the radio. No emergency had arisen during the trip, so he had sent no messages to base, but he was monitoring the transmitters in England which broadcast updated weather reports and warnings to the bomber force. Les was also listening to the German radio traffic. Any particularly strong signals, including certain known code words, would warn him that a night-fighter was getting too close.

The Canadian, Bob Adamson, his job done, stood behind Selwyn on the flight deck. His task now was to keep watch for other aircraft, friendly and unfriendly. Bill Hewson and Victor Osterloh would be gently swinging their turrets from side to side, keeping the hydraulic fluid warm and searching for any approaching night-fighter, but there was always the risk of collision with another Lancaster.

From time to time, the surrounding darkness was splashed by the tracer and flames of a combat, and yet another bomber began its final descent, but 'Victor' was left in peace for the first two hours after leaving Berlin.

It was about this time that Wilhelm Herget and his crew began working their way into the bomber stream. All aircraft at Florennes had remained on the ground during the early hours of the evening. With a strong wind blowing from the north west, the Bf 110's limited range and slow speed would have made it impossible for his unit to join the rush to the Heligoland Bight. Now the situation had changed. The bombers were not only flying directly towards his home base, they were also struggling against the same wind which had earlier boosted their approach to Berlin. Several hundred 'Tommies' were crawling across the map of Southern Germany and Luxembourg and he felt sure that at least one of them would be his.

There is little purpose in dwelling upon the events inside OL-V 'Victor' once Herget made his attack. The impact must have been shocking in its suddenness and its violence. It might be that all of Selwyn's crew died instantly. The evidence of Paulin Mathot, however, suggests that they did not. It will be recalled that four of the bodies which he saw were wearing parachutes. Only one member of the crew would have had a parachute attached to his harness before the attack, and that was the pilot, Selwyn. The others would have needed to leave their stations and remove the 'chutes from stowage racks before clipping them on. This was a particularly difficult manoeuvre for the rear gunner. His parachute pack was located inside the fuselage. He was obliged to wriggle backwards, through the sliding turret doors, to reach it. When Bill Hewson was found beside Monsieur Jacques' house, his parachute was in place, clipped to the harness. So what did happen?

We can only surmise that, although fatally damaged, 'Victor' was initially still flyable. Selwyn will have given the order to bail out, and at least three of his comrades made ready to do so. Flying Officer D E Tolley, an Australian flight engineer who was flying that night in another 83 Squadron Lancaster, wrote to Dorothy a few days later with what he hoped would be an encouraging letter. He told her that he had seen 'Victor' going down in 'a controlled descent'. Whether or not this was true, it may well have been so. But that control must have been soon lost, otherwise one or more of the men would have jumped. It seems likely that the flying controls were so badly damaged that Selwyn could not hold the aircraft in a stable attitude. Once it began to spin, he would have had no hope of recovery.

The Lancaster was undoubtedly an excellent design but, from the crews' point of view, it had two disadvantages. The location of the forward escape hatch and the main door prevented seven men from leaving the aircraft in a hurry, and the interior had a tendency to burn. Everything in Paulin Mathot's account indicates that 'Victor' went out of control soon after being hit and began to spin, that a small fire broke out inside the fuselage, and centrifugal force then prevented any member of the crew from reaching either of the two exits. The result was a foregone conclusion. The spin became ever more violent and the aircraft broke up in mid-air. The orderly line of debris, stretching in a direct 900 metres line from the Jacques house to the far edge of Sautour village, indicates that the final airframe failure occurred at an altitude of no more than 1500 feet.

On the morning of 28 January, a clerk at Wyton typed out the latest pages for the Squadron Operational Record. Beside the entry for OL-V 'Victor', she wrote: 'Nothing heard from this aircraft after take-off'. Those solemn words were to be the only epitaph for Selwyn Alcock and his crew until 1990 when the search for an answer began.

Missing

Late in the afternoon of 28 January, the doorbell rang at Brockmoor Vicarage. It was the caller dreaded by every wartime family — a GPO telegram boy. The message was simple: 'Deeply regret to inform you that Flight Lieutenant S H Alcock RAFVR is reported missing from air operations over enemy territory'.

When several weeks passed without further news, Dorothy Alcock decided to contact the Red Cross. She wrote to Geneva, explaining that her husband had failed to return from an operation in January and asking if any details could be traced. The IRC contacted the German authorities in, ironically, Berlin. After some months, Dorothy received a letter from Geneva which dashed any last hope that Selwyn might be alive, perhaps a prisoner of war or under the protection of the Resistance.

The Germans confirmed that an officer wearing identity tags with the name S H Alcock had been interred at Florennes on 29 January. The letter was a crushing blow for Dorothy and for Selwyn's parents. The health of all of them declined, Dorothy having three years away from any kind of employment and the Reverend Alcock dying of consumption in 1949.

The crew of OL-V 'Victor' lay undisturbed at Jusaine-Rosée, on the perimeter of Florennes airfield, for the next three years. During this time, in early September 1944, the Allies over-ran the area following their breakout from the Normandy beach-head. The base was taken over by the United States Army Air Force. Following the return of peace, it was transferred to the Belgian Air Force and the decision was made to expand it as part of the NATO defence system. The new breed of fast jets needed longer runways, so it became necessary to exhume all the bodies at Jusaine-Rosée. The Germans and Americans made their own arrangements, the British moved their dead to the Commonwealth War Graves Commission cemetery at Hotton, thirty miles to the east and deep in the beautiful wooded hills of the

Displayed at the RAF Museum, Hendon, is the sole surviving intact Wellington (MF628, a Mark X, built in 1944). Also at Hendon is one of a handful of surviving examples of the mighty Lancaster (R5868, a Mark Ib, built in 1942). Allocated to 83 Sqn with the call-sign OL-Q 'Queenie', it was regularly flown by F/Lt F J Garvey until, after 67 sorties, it was transferred to 467 Sqn at RAF Bottesford. With a new call-sign, PO-S 'Sugar' it continued in front-line service until the end of the war and completed 137 sorties in total.

Ardennes. The formal reinterment took place on 27 May 1947.

The years rolled by. Selwyn's great friend, Norman Mackie, had returned to active service, gained a second DFC in recognition of his escape from Switzerland, and later a DSO for his work with 571 Squadron, based at RAF Oakington. This unit was equipped with Mosquito light bombers and formed part of Bomber Command's Light Night Striking Force. By war's end, Norman had completed the astonishing total of ninety-two operations. He made a permanent career in the Royal Air Force, married in 1958, and retired in the rank of Wing Commander in 1967.

Selwyn's widow, Dorothy, returned to her home town of Torquay. In late 1944, accompanied by her mother and Selwyn's parents, she attended an Investiture at Buckingham Palace to receive from the hands of King George VI the DFC awarded posthumously to her husband. Some years later she remarried and now has two fine daughters and three grandchildren.

In Australia, Betty Hewson also remarried and rebuilt her life. She raised Bill's infant sons and in due course they made successful careers for themselves, Alan as an engineer and John as a surgeon. In Canada, the Adamsons moved away from Innisfree and, as the surviving four children grew to adulthood, scattered themselves across that vast country. Memories faded, the hurt went away, and life, for those involved, went on.

The Belgians, the villagers of Sautour, were in many ways those who had least cause to mourn the deaths of the 'Victor' crew. It was, after all, no more than blind chance which brought the Lancaster crashing down beside their homes. It might as easily have come to earth at any one of a thousand other such small communities in Western Europe. The local people had no ties of blood or friendship with its crew. It is the village of Sautour, however, which has done most to preserve in tangible form the events of 27 January 1944.

Aux Memoires des Equipages

Selwyn Alcock, Bill Hewson, Eric Sargent, Bob Adamson, Norman Mackie — these were among the hundreds of aircrew who flew over Western Europe during the early years of the war. They were followed by thousands more. While the pioneers were finishing their first tours, or falling to disaster, young men from all over the British Commonwealth were preparing to take their places. From the basic training stations and elementary flying schools in Canada, Rhodesia and South Africa, they came to England to advance their skills at the operational training units. For most of these new crews, a leaflet-dropping sortie over France or Belgium was their first tentative incursion into enemy air space and the final stage of preparation before being posted to a front-line bomber squadron. The code-word for such trips was 'nickel'.

At nineteen minutes to eleven o'clock on the evening of 27 April 1942, a Wellington twin-engined bomber of No 27 Operational Training Unit left the runway at RAF Lichfield, not far from Wolverhampton. On board were five trainee aircrew, all holding the lowest flying rank of Sergeant, and all taut with anticipation. Tonight would put them to the test of crossing the English Channel for the first time. Their task was to fly independently over two or three French and Belgian cities and to release packets of leaflets. The texts were messages of hope and encouragement to the occupied peoples of those countries, assuring them that they were not forgotten. In theory, it was a simple and not particularly dangerous mission. It would give 'the new boys' confidence in themselves as a team, spiced with an element of risk.

Exactly what happened aboard this aircraft will never be known, but it is certain that the navigation was at fault. The planned route should have been completed in little more than three hours. Arrangements had been made for the Wellington to be refuelled as soon as it landed back at Lichfield in the early hours so that another fledgling crew could take it on a practice cross-country flight to York, the Isle of Man and back to Lichfield. In the event, five-and-a-quarter hours after take-off, it was still tracking over Southern Belgium.

Even over the lightly-defended countryside of Belgium, a lonely wandering enemy aircraft was bound to attract German attention. South of the industrial city of Charleroi, it had the misfortune to pass over a Luftwaffe searchlight unit. This battery, ABT 118, caught the Wellington in a web of brilliant beams and held it, trapped, while a night-fighter closed in for 'the kill'. The fighter, thought to have been a Bf 110 operating from a base at Laon, Northern France, had been hunting for precisely this sort of easy target. No doubt the British pilot turned and dived and followed the rules of evasion he had been taught, but he had little chance of escape. A burst of cannon fire sent him down in a steep dive and he smashed into a small field on the edge of Sautour.

There were many German troops, from a wireless relay station, billeted in and around Sautour at that time. Although it was four o'clock in the morning, numbers of them came hurrying to the crash site. Some formed a cordon around the wreckage, others stood watching the flames and cheering. A short while later the aircraft's main fuel tanks exploded, killing or injuring eighteen of the German spectators.

It was the habit of an amiable elderly soldier to visit the local farms each day to purchase fresh milk. On the morning following the crash, he revealed that the 'English' airmen had all been killed and their bodies taken away for burial at Charleroi. Several of the village's young people went to their priest and suggested that a Mass for the dead should be held in the local church and a memorial cross erected at the crash site. Apart from wishing to express their respect for the unknown airmen, they wanted to demonstrate their opposition to their German occupiers.

The village carpenter was ill and unable to work, so the job of making the cross was given to Camille Bayot in the neighbouring village of Vodecée. Word was passed quietly around that a Mass would be held on the following Tuesday. This information reached the Germans, and the priest was promptly arrested and imprisoned. His flock nevertheless gathered in the church and prayed for the souls of the Wellington's crew.

Meanwhile, Camille Bayot's cross had been taken under cover of darkness and hidden in a ditch near the wreckage. Marie Deville and one of her daughters kept watch on the patrolling sentries while Arthur Deville and Jules Penet crept along the ditch. It was their intention to erect it on the morning of the Mass and to defy the Germans with this surprise gesture.

On Tuesday, a group of twenty brave villagers approached the barriers surrounding the wreck. Jules Penet retrieved the cross from its hiding place and drove it into the ground while the others prayed and laid wreaths. One woman, Madame Anais Piot, ignored the sentries' shouts and threw her wreath over the barrier towards the wreck. She was arrested, and her husband was obliged to borrow 150 Reichsmarks to pay for her release. Over the following days the Germans removed the debris and cleared the site, but they left the cross. Later it disappeared, removed possibly by soldiers or by a collaborator, but it was soon replaced at the instigation of Madame Piot. This memorial remained in place for many years, but its condition gradually deteriorated under the impact of wind and rain. It finally succumbed when a tractor accidentally collided with it.

In 1986, at the suggestion of Michel Putzeys, the local people agreed to commission the making of a new cross. The initiative was entirely their own and the cost was met from their own pockets. It was carried through without any official support from either the Belgian or British national authorities, indeed without them being informed of what was planned. To quote one of them, Franz Wilmot: 'We knew nothing of these men other than the fact that they had died while trying to give us our liberty. It was our way of thanking all twelve men, the five from the Wellington in 1942, and the seven from the Lancaster in 1944, for their sacrifice on our behalf. This was nothing to do with the authorities. It was the voice of Sautour which was speaking'.

On 11 May 1986, the new cross, two metres high and finely carved in oak, was dedicated and blessed by the local priest. Amongst the attending crowd were the Mayor and a small invited party of Belgian Air Force officers from Florennes air base. A Union Jack, draped over the memorial plaque, was lifted to reveal the wording: *Aux Memoires des Equipages de la RAF, Tombés en Combat, 1942-1944.** It was a simple ceremony and one which brought tears to the eyes of Jules Penet. Forty-four years earlier, he had risked his liberty, if not his life, to erect that first cross under the noses of the German sentries.

---

*To the memory of the RAF crews, fallen in combat, 1942-1944

To the outsider, who did not share the experiences of wartime occupation and later liberation, the continuing respect for our dead by the people of this quiet corner of rural Belgium can be viewed only with a sense of wonder. Their dedication becomes even more impressive when one looks at the price which they too paid for their freedom.

On 24 January 1944, the nearby hamlet of Sart-en-Fagne was struck by a terrible tragedy. The Americans had mounted a daylight raid on Eschweiler, near Aachen. A formation of B-17 Flying Fortresses of the USAAF 8th Air Force was flying from East Anglia with an enormous escort of 678 fighters — Mustangs and Thunderbolts. The intention was to provoke the Luftwaffe into accepting the challenge and thereby inflict heavy losses on it. The Germans reacted by sending up large numbers of their day fighters and a series of dog-fights broke out along the bombers' route.

As normal when engaged by enemy aircraft, the Americans jettisoned their long-range fuel tanks as they went into action. One of these tanks, still half full of petrol, spiralled down from thirty thousand feet and crashed squarely through the roof of the village school. The lady teacher and her nine pupils were all burned to death. Their ages were seven to twelve. The total population of Sart-en-Fagne was one hundred and fifty. An entire generation of children was taken from them.

The mass funeral for 'les petites victimes' and their teacher was held on the morning of 27 January. Twelve hours later, Selwyn Alcock and his crew fell from that same deadly sky.

The Boys from Blenheim

By a curious coincidence, Wellington Z8901 which crashed at Sautour carried the same call-sign as Selwyn Alcock's Lancaster — 'V Victor'. Its five man crew was equally representative of Bomber Command's worldwide recruitment. As 'Bomber' Harris pointed out later, in his memoirs, the Dominions and Colonies provided forty percent of his aircrew and forty-nine per cent of his pilots.

Two of the Wellington's crew were New Zealanders, one an Australian. Recent contact with their surviving relatives and friends has served to illustrate the quality of the young men who voluntarily travelled halfway around the globe to serve their King and Empire.

Arthur Greer was born on a large sheep station in Western Queensland. His father was the manager and he had two brothers and two sisters, all of whom are still living. There were no schools within several hundred miles in any direction, so the children spent most of their younger days at boarding schools. Arthur, or 'Bill' as he was always known, was educated by the Christian Brothers at Mount Carmel and later at the Agricultural College at Ingham. With his brother, Murray, he then worked in the canefields of Northern Queensland before going back to sheep farming, as a 'jackaroo', in 1938. As soon as war broke out, he volunteered for service in the Royal Australian Air Force. After training in Canada as a wireless operator, he arrived in England in late 1941 and was posted to No 27 OTU, RAF Lichfield. With him were two New Zealanders — Wilfred Mutton, a trainee bomb aimer, and Eric Inder, a trainee air gunner.

Little is known of Wilfred Mutton other than having been a quiet, well-spoken young man. His parents lived in Johnsonville, Wellington, but recent enquiries have failed to trace any surviving relatives. Official records show that he was educated at Wellington Technical College and, after leaving school, was employed by a local firm of radio manufacturers, Collier & Beale. He also began a part-time course in radio technology with the International Correspondence Schools, but abandoned this to volunteer as an airman. After initial training at Levin, he embarked for Canada in September 1940 aboard the SS *Awatea*. Training at Calgary, Alberta, and McDonald, Manitoba, resulted in promotion to Sergeant as a Wireless Operator Air Gunner, or 'WOP/AG' as his trade was usually known. Sailing from Halifax, Nova Scotia, he attended a refresher course at No 1 Signals School, Cranwell, before moving to No 27 OTU at Lichfield in November 1941. The next five months were devoted to training flights, practice bombing and aerial gunnery with his new crew. He was twenty-one years of age, a bachelor, when he died.

Eric Inder's forebears had emigrated to New Zealand in 1855 from the Somerset village of Martock. His father had fought with the 1st NZEF (New Zealand Expeditionary Force) in the war of 1914-1918. His brother, Leicester, followed their father's example by joining the 2nd NZEF in 1939 and fought in the battle for Crete. He then spent four years in a prison camp in Austria before returning to his native Blenheim in 1945.

Eric decided instead to be an airman. Unmarried, at thirty-one much older than his fellow trainees, he was a carpenter by trade. He had been educated at Marlborough College, Blenheim. Employed by J Hamitt, a local building firm, he gave his spare time to training with the Marlborough Mounted Rifles as a machine-gunner Trooper. He volunteered for war service with the RNZAF within days of Hitler's invasion of Poland and sailed for Canada in October 1940 in the SS *Aorangi*. Like hundreds of other Commonwealth trainees, he passed through the vast production line of the Empire Air Training Scheme before taking ship for England in May 1941 as a Sergeant Air Gunner. The sole surviving member of his family — his brother Leicester — remembers Eric as having been 'an active outdoor sort of man'.

A great friend of Eric had similarly travelled from Blenheim to Canada and then to England and No 27 OTU. He was Geoff Gane, and the two of them were known as 'the Blenheim boys'. Geoff recalls that night when Eric was lost: 'Our crew were waiting for the Wellington to return from its leaflet raid so that we could do one of our last cross-country training flights. The machine didn't turn up as

Sgt Eric Inder, Royal New
Zealand Air Force, the rear
gunner from Blenheim.

Sgt Arthur 'Bill' Greer, Royal
Australian Air Force, the wireless
operator from Queensland.

*A Wellington Mark II of 104 Sqn operating from RAF Driffield in mid-1941. Known
affectionately as the 'Wimpey', the type was Bomber Command's workhorse until
gradually replaced by the new 'heavies' – the Manchester, Stirling, Halifax
and Lancaster.*

planned at two in the morning, so we snuck off to bed. We never found out what happened, but we guessed it was a night-fighter'.

Geoff Gane had only marginally better luck than Eric. He and his crew were posted to 12 Squadron, RAF Binbrook. They arrived in time to take part in the first of the great 'thousand bomber raids', the attack on Cologne on 30 May 1942. They were amongst the forty-three crews to be lost that night. Their Wellington was set on fire. Geoff took to his parachute and spent the next three years as a prisoner of war.

For the reasons mentioned earlier, it is not possible to obtain details of the two Englishmen who died with their Australian and New Zealand friends at Sautour. The captain of the Wellington, the pilot, was Sergeant George Dale. He was the son of Frederick and Edith Dale, of Hanwell, Middlesex, and he was nineteen years old. His navigator, Sergeant Walter Jewell, was the son of Walter and Maud Jewell, of West Ealing, and he was twenty-one. Their names are to be found on their headstones in the tranquil corner of the Charleroi Communal Cemetery reserved for Commonwealth War Graves Commission burials, and on a roll of honour which now hangs in the chancel of Sautour village church.

Remembrance

In February 1991, the author of this book was motoring through Belgium on holiday. Knowing that Selwyn Alcock's Lancaster had crashed somewhere in the vicinity, he went to Florennes and asked the staff at the Town Hall if they had any knowledge of that long-ago incident. He was referred to a local school-teacher, Roland Charlier, who was compiling a history of the nearby air base established by the Germans in 1942. Their first encounter was unforgettable.

'Good evening. I'm interested in a Lancaster bomber which came down somewhere around here in January 1944'. 'Ah yes, Flight Lieutenant Alcock. How can I help?'. 'Well, perhaps I can help you. Here is a photograph of Alcock'. 'Good, most useful. And here is a photograph of the pilot who shot him down. His name was Herget'.

Few researchers can hope to savour such a golden moment of mutual discovery. It was at that first meeting that the existence of the Sautour memorial cross became known to anyone from outside the immediate locality. This book is the result of the in-depth enquiries which flowed from that initial contact. They culminated, a year later, on 23 February 1992, with an extraordinary act of remembrance.

On a cold damp Sunday, the people of Sautour gathered in their church to attend a Mass at which they prayed for the souls of the dead airmen. A uniquely Roman Catholic event, it mirrored the occasion when, in 1942, they had defied their

23 February 1992, a day of remembrance for the people of Sautour. Gathered at the cross are (left to right): Jules Penet, Mde Anais Piot, Michel Putzeys, Roger Perkins, Norman Mackie, Franz Wilmot, Lionel Digby. The village has changed little over the years.

occupiers by gathering to pray for Sergeant George Dale and his four comrades. Many members of the congregation had been present then as young men and young women on the threshold of life. Franz Wilmot, Paulin Mathot, Michel Putzeys, Désiré Jacques, Jules Penet, Anais Piot. 'They shall grow not old as we that are left grow old'. The true cost of warfare, the loss of youth and flowering talents, could not have been more sadly reflected than in the faces of these gentle Belgian country folk.

Addressing them in French, Wing Commander Norman Mackie, DSO, DFC and bar, spoke of his gratitude to the villagers for their dedication, over half a century, to preserving the memory of the twelve fallen airmen. He spoke of the gratitude felt by countless former Allied aircrew who, having been shot down, were guided to safety, at enormous risk to themselves, by members of the Resistance movement. And lastly, he spoke of Selwyn, his long lost friend. There were more than a few tears in the church that morning. Being of the same generation, having witnessed the same great events in history, Norman Mackie represented something which the villagers could recognise in themselves.

At the conclusion of his speech, Norman formally presented to Franz Wilmot, as representative of the community, an illuminated scroll commemorating the seven former members of 83 Squadron. With it was a plaque bearing the Squadron crest, both items having been prepared and sent over from England by Ron Low and Frank Harper, archivists and historians of 83 Squadron. Together with a large portrait of Selwyn Alcock and a roll of honour naming both crews, they will remain in the church in perpetuity.

Following the ceremonies in Sautour church, Norman Mackie laid a wreath, on behalf of the Royal Air Force, at the village memorial which commemorates the local boys who fell in both world wars. A similar ceremony was then held at the memorial cross erected in 1986 and described earlier. A Royal British Legion poppy wreath, with the RAF device at its centre, was laid on behalf of the twelve surviving families of the Commonwealth airmen who died at this place.

The tensions and emotions of the morning were released at a luncheon given by our Belgian hosts and which lasted all afternoon. As the courses came and went, as the wine thawed the restraints of formality, wartime adventures were recalled ever more freely and with growing hilarity. The Englishmen present found that they could speak French more fluently than they had thought possible. The Belgians remembered words and phrases in English last used in their school days. Bonds of friendship were forged which will not easily be broken. And underlying the ceremonies and discussions of the day was the feeling that, somehow, these people had been released from a self-imposed duty. For more than half a lifetime, for all that they knew, they alone had preserved a memory. Now it was shared, and so, finally, laid to rest.

Hotton War Cemetery. Paulin Mathot (left) and Franz Wilmot (right) lay a single red rose at the headstone of each of the seven Lancaster crew. Below, the memorials presented to the people of Sautour by the survivors of 83 Squadron.

Appendix A

The following is the text (the original being in French) of the memorial which now hangs in Sautour church:

This plaque is presented to the people of Sautour
by wartime members of No 83 (Pathfinder) Squadron
of the Royal Air Force
to mark our eternal gratitude for honouring the memory of
our former comrades

Flight Lieutenant S H Alcock DFC RAF(VR)	*Pilot*
Sergeant S Bullamore RAF(VR)	*Flight Engineer*
Flight Lieutenant E W Sargent DFC RAF(VR)	*Navigator*
Flying Officer R H Adamson RCAF	*Bomb Aimer*
Flight Lieutenant L C Davis RAF(VR)	*Wireless Operator*
Warrant Officer V G Osterloh RAF(VR)	*Air Gunner*
Flight Lieutenant W H Hewson RAAF	*Air Gunner*

They gave their lives for our freedom whilst returning from
an operation against Berlin, on 27 January 1944

The new memorial cross erected on 11 May 1986 by the inhabitants of Sautour
honours not only the memory of the Lancaster crew listed above, but also the
crew of a Wellington bomber which crashed nearby, on 28 April 1942

Sergeant G A Dale RAF(VR)	*Pilot*
Sergeant W J Jewell RAF(VR)	*Navigator*
Sergeant A W Greer RAAF	*Wireless Operator*
Sergeant W G Mutton RNZAF	*Bomb Aimer*
Sergeant E C Inder RNZAF	*Air Gunner*

The seven graves of the Lancaster crew are in the
Commonwealth War Graves Commission cemetery at Hotton.
The five graves of the Wellington crew are in the
Communal Cemetery of Charleroi
PER ARDUA AD ASTRA

Appendix B

Casualties

The following is a list of aircrew who flew with Alcock on various occasions and who, like him, did not survive.

First tour — Hampdens

F/Lt A G Mills DFC (pilot)	Buried at Scampton (20.08.1941)
Sgt C W Allen (air gunner)	No known grave (02.09.1941)
Sgt H F Kay (air gunner)	Harlingen War Cemetery, Holland (02.09.1941)
F/O W C Rasberry (air gunner)	Hannover War Cemetery (14.08.1941)

Note: it is possible that others who had served with him were lost later while serving with other squadrons (having completed their first tours with 83 Sqn).

Second tour — Lancasters

F/Sgt R Ellwood (wireless operator)	Berlin War Cemetery (02.01.1944)
F/Sgt K E L Farmelo (flight engineer)	Berlin War Cemetery (20.01.1944)
F/Sgt D J Phelon (wireless operator)	Berlin War Cemetery (20.01.1944)
F/Sgt R A Adams DFM (air gunner)	Berlin War Cemetery (20.01.1944)
F/Sgt E D MacPherson DFM (air gunner)	Berlin War Cemetery (20.01.1944)
F/Sgt F E Burton-Burgess (flight engineer)	Berlin War Cemetery (23.11.1943)
Sgt R Richardson (flight engineer)	Berlin War Cemetery (22.01.1944)
Sgt W S Travers (flight engineer)	Berlin War Cemetery (20.01.1944)

Note: F/Lt R King DFC, with whom Alcock had flown his first Lancaster sortie on 22 September 1943, was the only survivor when JB461 exploded over Berlin on 20 January 1944. His left arm was amputated and he suffered other serious injuries. After some time in a prison camp, he was repatriated to England under the auspices of the International Red Cross in exchange for an injured German prisoner of war.

Appendix C

Hampden losses

The following is a list of every Hampden in which Alcock ever flew, on operational sorties, and each aircraft's eventual fate.

X3144   Flew into the sea of the Friesian Islands, 02.09.1941. All four crew killed.

AD934   Windscreen iced up. Crashed at Swanton Morley, 22.10.1941. Crew unhurt.

AD935   Hit a tree, 14.08.1941. Two crew killed, one injured, one unhurt.

AE131   Hit by flak, crashed near Hanover, 14.08.1941. All four crew killed.

AE133   Crashed at Kampen (Sylt) after engine failure, 10.01.1942. Two crew killed, two POW.

X3061   Transferred to 44 Sqn, then 420 Sqn, then 14 OTU, then 415 (Torpedo) Sqn. Written off after being hit by another aircraft on the ground.

AE363   Transferred to 144 (Torpedo) Sqn, then 5 OTU, then 32 OTU, then moved to Canada. Struck off charge (scrapped), April 1944.

AD870   Transferred to 408 (Torpedo) Sqn. Scrapped February 1944.

AE364   Transferred to 144 (Torpedo) Sqn, then 5 OTU. Scrapped, May 1944.

AT127   Crashed at Sedgebrook, Lincolnshire, 09.01.1942. Crew unhurt.

Appendix D

Lancaster losses

The following is a list of every Lancaster in which Alcock ever flew, on operational sorties, and each aircraft's eventual fate.

JB352   *OL-C*. Shot down on a Berlin raid, 30.01.1944. Pilot, F/Lt A H S Sambridge. Six crew killed, one POW.

JB461   *OL-L*. Shot down over Berlin, 20.01.1944. Six crew killed, one POW.

JA705   *OL-M*. Several major raids with 83 Sqn, then transferred to 617 Sqn in 1944 for training purposes. Struck off (scrapped) in 1947.

JB309   *OL-N*. Transferred to 207 Sqn, then to a Heavy Conversion Unit. This was the much repaired veteran 'Nan' in which Alcock had so many misadventures during the winter of 1943-1944. It survived the war and was scrapped in 1947.

JB114   *OL-Q*. Survived six Berlin raids before going down on the seventh, 01.01.1944. F/Lt L W Munro and his crew all killed following a mid-air collision over Zehrensdorf (near Berlin).

JB402   *OL-R*. Shot down on the Mailly-le-Camp raid, 03.05.1944, with eight crew on board. Pilot, S/Ldr E N M Sparks. Seven evaded, one POW.

JA967   *OL-S*. Flew on all the Berlin raids before being lost on 27.01.1944 (the same night that Alcock was lost). Seven crew killed.

ED601   *OL-T*. Shot down on a Berlin raid, 02.12.1943, having been transferred to 203 Sqn and given the new call-sign EM-N. The pilot, P/O A Mann, and his crew 'missing in action'.

JB724   *OL-V*. This was the aircraft captained by Alcock when he went down at Sautour on 27.01.1944.

In addition, he took part in training flights in two other Lancasters of 83 Sqn.

JA940   *OL-T*. Crashed on landing, 29.01.1944. Damaged beyond repair.

JB344   *OL-O*. Crashed on landing, Wyton, 17.12.1943 (Black Thursday). This was the aircraft captained by F E McClean as mentioned in the narrative.

Alcock's rear gunner, Bill Hewson, flew on training and operational sorties with five other different pilots in September 1943. An analysis of the later careers of their aircraft reveals a similar pattern of attrition.

JA712   *OL-B*. An exceptionally long serving machine. First operated by 7 Sqn, then transferred to 83 Sqn in July 1943, then to 550 Sqn as BQ-O in February 1844. Lost on a mission to Aachen, 27.05.1944.

JA701   *OL-E*. Took part in the three big Hamburg raids and the Peenemunde attack. Lost during the Leipzig raid of 20.10.1943.

ED602   *OL-F*. Formerly with 467 (Australian) Sqn, flew on the three Hamburg raids and the Peenemunde raid with 83 Sqn, transferred to 619 Sqn in September 1944. Lost over Karlsruhe, 26.09.1944.

ED908   *OL-J*. An 83 Sqn veteran, transferred to 15 Sqn, lost over the Foret du Croc during the daylight raid of 20.07.1944.

EE201   *OL-N*. Rebuilt after the Mannheim raid of 23.09.1943, allocated a new call-sign, OL-D. Later transferred to a training unit. Struck off charge in 1945.

Les Davis, Alcock's wireless operator, had served with 83 Sqn for longer than any other man in that crew. His sorties with W/Cdr Searby and F/Lt Garvey have been noted in the narrative. Again, a survey of other aircraft in which he flew serves to confirm the extreme hazards of service in Bomber Command.

W4982   *OL-O*. One of the last Mark I Lancasters to be built. Lost over Mulheim, 22.06.1943.

W4953   *OL-W*. Another veteran Mark I. Transferred to 1656 Heavy Conversion Unit in August 1942, lost in a crash in November.

JA928   *OL-W*. Flown by W/Cdr Searby as Master Bomber on the Peenemunde raid. Lasted for the exceptionally long time of eight months before being shot down near Schweinfurt, 26.04.1944. All seven crew killed.

Appendix E

83 Squadron losses — Belgium, 1939-1945

Apart from Alcock's OL-V, the Squadron lost five other aircraft over Belgium during the course of the war. They are listed below.

21.04.1941 — Hampden OL-R X3119 — target Mannheim
F/Sgt R B Hanner (pilot), Sgt F A Whitehead (navigator), Sgt J B Ronnie (wireless operator), Sgt E S Phillips (air gunner).
The aircraft was operating from RAF SCAMPTON and crashed at HOUTHULST.
All four crew are buried in the local churchyard.

31.08.1941 — Hampden OL-O AD859 — target COLOGNE
Sgt F Dacey (pilot), Sgt G G Bensley (navigator), Sgt H G Tonks (wireless operator), Sgt J A D Clark (air gunner).
The aircraft was operating from RAF SCAMPTON and crashed at MUNSTERBILSEN.
All four crew are buried at HAVERLEE War Cemetery.

25.03.1942 — Manchester OL-H L7465 — target ESSEN
Sgt P Markides (pilot), P/O C H Danielsen (co-pilot), P/O D McConochie (navigator), Sgt A Woodcock (bomb aimer), Sgt T H Miller (wireless operator), Sgt A G Jaye (mid-upper gunner), Sgt C C Smith (rear gunner).
The aircraft was operating from RAF SCAMPTON and crashed at LICHAERT.
All seven crew are buried at HAVERLEE War Cemetery.

25.08.1942 — Lancaster OL-G R5610 — target FRANKFURT
F/Lt O R Matheson DFC (pilot), F/O J W Dicker (navigator), F/Sgt W R Cubberley (wireless operator), Sgt P Squires (flight engineer), F/Lt R M Buchan DFC (navigator), Sgt H D Quintrell (mid-upper gunner), Sgt E T Norman (rear gunner).
The aircraft was operating from RAF WYTON and crashed at NORKHOVEN.
The pilot, Matheson, evaded capture and returned to England. Dicker and Cubberley both survived and were taken prisoner. The other four are buried at NORKHOVEN Communal Cemetery.
F/Lt Buchan was Staff Navigation Officer to the Pathfinder Force.

11.04.1944 — Lancaster OL-A ND389 — target AACHEN
P/O V McConnell (pilot), Sgt T Powell (flight engineer), F/O A J Watts (navigator), F/Sgt H S Vickers (bomb aimer), Sgt W Surgey (wireless operator), Sgt G W Bradshaw (mid-upper gunner), Sgt W J Throsby (rear gunner).
The aircraft was operating from RAF WYTON and crashed at BELISE.
All seven crew are buried at SCHOONSELHOF Cemetery.

Appendix F

Major Wilhelm Herget

He was born in Stuttgart on 30 June 1910. In May 1939 he joined the German Air Force (Luftwaffe) as a trainee pilot and qualified early in the following year. He was physically well adapted for the confined space of a contemporary fighter cockpit, being no more than five feet and five inches in height.

He commenced operational flying in the Spring of 1940 and destroyed two Allied aircraft during the invasion of France. His unit then took part in the Battle of Britain and he shot down ten RAF fighters, all by day, during that period.

In 1941 he converted to night-fighters, flying the twin-engined Messerschmitt Bf 110. In July he destroyed two Blenheim light bombers while serving with NJG3, but was then transferred to Iraq. He was attached to II/ZG76, a fighter-bomber group operating in Iraqi Air Force colours and deployed to support local insurgents. Iraq was at that time partially under British administration, but Germany was trying hard to support nationalist groups sympathetic to the Nazi cause. Iraq's oilfields, and the route to India, were the stakes for which both sides were playing.

Herget was based at Raschid airfield, but his unit had few clashes with the larger RAF force based at Habbaniyah. He scored no more victories during his time in the Middle East. After an absence of eight months he returned to Western Europe in April 1942. Responding to the steady increase in the RAF's bombing campaign over Germany, the Luftwaffe was creating a chain of radar stations and fighter bases from Denmark down into Northern France. An element of the expansion programme was the construction of a major night-fighter base at Florennes. Several thousand forced labourers and German technicians were building a permanent all-weather runway, two kilometres in length, and all the facilities to support a group of forty Bf 110s. The new unit was numbered I/NJG/4 and Herget was appointed the commanding officer. Over the next two years, based at Florennes, he became one of Germany's top-scoring opponents of the British night bombers.

The list of his victories is a catalogue of the types of aircraft deployed over North West Europe between 1942 and the end of the war: Hampdens, Wellingtons, Stirlings, Halifaxes and, above all, Lancasters. Additionally, he shot down at least one American B-17 Flying Fortress and, at the end of the war, a USAAF Thunderbolt.

While some of the Luftwaffe's pilots never truly mastered the complex business of getting behind a bomber, unseen, and making a successful attack, Herget was one of the deadly few who could fly in the worst weather conditions and shoot down two or three bombers in rapid succession. His first multiple success came on the night of 10/11 April 1943. He caught two homeward-bound

OFW
Emil Große

Herget (right) and his well-practiced crew. Awarded the Knight's Cross, he is congratulated by Adolf Hitler while Herman Goering, head of the Luftwaffe, looks on approvingly.

Wellingtons and destroyed both in the space of thirty-two minutes. On 17 April, seventeen minutes apart, he shot down a Lancaster and a Halifax returning from their distant target in Pilsen, Czechoslovakia. On 22 June, over Holland, he brought down two Lancasters and a Wellington.

He continued to score single victories on a regular basis throughout 1943, but his next major sortie was the night of 26/27 November. This was the Berlin raid which marked Selwyn Alcock's elevation to the status of a 'backer-up'. Herget shot down three inward-bound Lancasters in rapid succession, landed, refuelled, took off again, and destroyed an outward-bound Halifax near St Vith.

It was the night of 20/21 December which saw Major Herget at the peak of his skill. This was a maximum effort by Bomber Command to hit Frankfurt, and the only occasion in his career when Selwyn Alcock turned back with engine failure. The bomber stream was heading towards the Ruhr Valley on a route which passed not far north of Herget's base at Florennes. He worked his way into the stream as it crossed the Rhine and, in the space of fifty minutes, shot down two Halifaxes and six Lancasters. It was a remarkable performance. The cost to the Luftwaffe was less than a thousand rounds of ammunition.

As a measure of his triumph, the RAF lost forty-one heavy bombers that night. This figure includes losses from all causes — flak, night-fighter attacks and accidents. Herget and his two crewmen had, on their own, inflicted twenty percent of the total damage.

He had other multiple successes in 1944, but never again matched his achievement of the Frankfurt raid. On June 1943, having scored his first thirty 'kills', he was awarded the Knight's Cross (Ritterkreuz). On 11 April 1944, having made 451 operational sorties and having been credited with sixty-three Allied aircraft, he gained the Knight's Cross with Oakleaves (Eichenlaub) and was personally congratulated by Hitler.

He commanded I/NJG/4 at Florennes until it was forced by the Allied advance, in late August 1944, to withdraw into Germany. In December he left the unit in order to learn to fly the revolutionary twin-jet Messerschmitt 262 day-fighter. The great German fighter leader, Adolf Galland, was forming a new unit, JV44, equipped with these powerful machines. His pilots, like himself, were veterans of the Luftwaffe's triumphant early years. Starved of fuel, harried on the ground, facing a blizzard of Allied aircraft every time they took to the air, this handful of pioneer jet pilots battled on to the end. Defeat for their country was now inevitable, they flew only to uphold the honour of the fighter arm.

Herget scored his last victory, his seventy-second, on 27 April 1945. Six days later, for the first time in his career, he was himself shot down. Flying a small communications aircraft, a Storch, he came down in flames near Miesbach and was taken prisoner. Three days later, Nazi Germany accepted unconditional surrender.

Following his release from prison camp, he commenced a career in publishing. He kept in touch with his former comrades and actively encouraged contact with their former opponents. He regularly visited the United Kingdom where he was welcomed by ex-Bomber Command aircrew who, in earlier years, would have viewed him in a very different light. In turn, he invited to his home some of those who, in wartime, he had tried hard to kill. The Munich episode, so vividly described by 'Hamish' Mahaddie in his Foreword to this book, captures to perfection the paradox of war and peace.

Wilhelm Herget was, by all accounts, a man of great charm and good humour. In 1974, at the age of sixty-four, he died following a heart attack in Switzerland. For what it may be worth, Selwyn Alcock had fallen to a worthy opponent.

Sources

Bibliography

There are many published accounts of the bombing campaign over North West Europe between 1939 and 1945, but the following have been of the greatest assistance to me in searching for both the fact and the spirit of Bomber Command in general and the Pathfinder Force in particular.

The Lancaster at War, in three volumes by Mike Garbett and Brian Goulding, 1971, 1979 and 1984

The Bomber Command War Diaries, by Martin Middlebrook and Chris Everitt, 1985

Bomber Battle for Berlin, by Group Captain John Searby, DSO, DFC, 1991

The Berlin Raids — RAF Bomber Command 1943-1944, by Martin Middlebrook, 1988

The Avro Lancaster, by Francis K Mason, 1989

Bomber, by Len Deighton, 1970

Archival sources

Public Record Office AIR 24/264, AIR 27/481, and AIR 27/686-688

Aircrew Flying Log (RCAF R.96), of Aust 411704 F/Lt W H Hewson RAAF

Personnel Management Centre, RAF Innsworth, Gloucester (UK)

HQ New Zealand Defence Force, Wellington (NZ)

Australian Defence Force, Canberra, ACT (Aust)

National Archives of Canada, Ottawa (Can)

The Municipal Administrator, Innisfree, Alberta (Can)

County Record Office, Chester (UK)

The Headmaster, Wells Cathedral School, Wells, Somerset (UK)

Examinations Officer, University of Durham (UK)

Commonwealth War Graves Commission, Maidenhead (UK)

Photographic illustrations

I am deeply obliged to the following for permission to use photographs from their archives or personal collections: Dorothy Murrell, Roland Charlier, W/Cdr Norman Mackie DSO, DFC, the Adamson family (Canada), the Greer and Hewson families (Australia), Leicester Inder (New Zealand), RAF Museum (Hendon), Pierre Wiave (Vers L'Avenir), Franz Wilmot, Frank Harper, Ron Low and Peter Green.

Acknowledgements

Finally, my thanks are due to all of those who assisted me with my researches:

in France and Belgium	Roland Charlier, Roger Antoine, Jean-Louis Roba, Franz Wilmot, Jules Penet, Désiré Jacques, Michel Putzeys, Paulin Mathot
in Canada	Pat Adamson, Andrea Stepanik
in Australia	Michael D'Arcy, Betty Hewson, John Hewson, Alan Hewson, Colin Rhead, Murray Greer
in New Zealand	Howard Chamberlain, Leicester Inder, Ross Inder, Geoff Gane
in the United Kingdom	Dorothy Murrell, Clifford Westwood, Brian Bosley, John Baxter, Fred Trethewey, Norman Mackie, Don Pidding, Hamish Mahaddie, Richard Humble

Particular thanks are due to Ron Low and Frank Harper. After twenty years of painstaking research, their unofficial history entitled *83 Squadron, 1917-1969,* is about to be published. Both were members of the Squadron, and they have created an immense archive of material relating to the individual services of their former comrades. I am indebted to them for having so generously permitted me to draw upon that archive.

Finally, and on behalf of the families who lost a loved one in Wellington 'V Victor' or Lancaster 'V Victor' at Sautour, a word of thanks to the staff of the Commonwealth War Graves Commission for their perpetual care of the graves at Charleroi and at Hotton.

Index